Song Of Meri-Khem

A Pilgrim's Journey

by
Judith Page

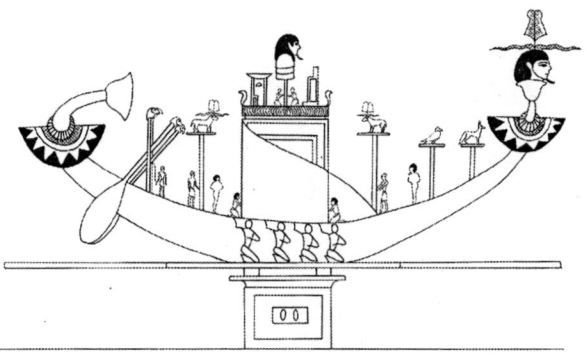

I dedicate this poem to Sir Kenneth Trezise OBE and the late Billie Walker John, who in life was a Universal Setian.

Song Of Meri-Khem

A Pilgrim's Journey

by Judith Page

Mandrake

Acknowledgements

I give grateful thanks to my cousin Sir Kenneth Trezise OBE, for his valuable assistance of this work, unlimited patience and guidance in the editing of this poem.

Finally I thank my daughter Miriam who has allowed me to use her image on the front cover. Her beauteous form matches her beauteous nature.

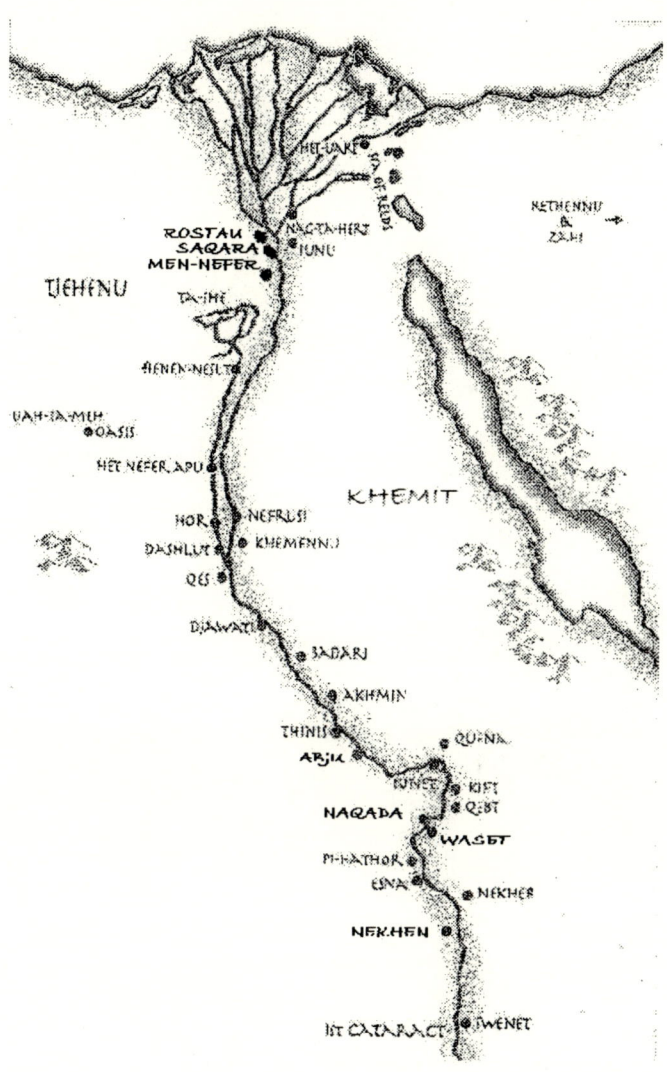

Khemit

Copyright © 2007 Mandrake & Judith Page

All rights reserved. No part of this work may be reproduced or utilized in any form by any means electronic or mechanical, including *xerography, photocopying, microfilm*, and *recording,* or by any information storage system without permission in writing from the publishers.

Published by
Mandrake of Oxford
PO Box 250
OXFORD
OX1 1AP (UK)

A CIP catalogue record for this book is available from the British Library and the US Library of Congress.

isbn 978-1869928-99-5

Contents

	List of illustrations	8
	Introduction	9
1	Pilgrimage	21
2	Journey to Nekhen	23
3	Journey to Naqada	27
4	Journey to Thebes (Waset)	33
5	Journey to Karnak	36
6	Journey to the Temple of Khonsu	37
7	Journey to the Temple of Luxor	47
8	Journey to Abydos (Abju)	55
9	The Rise of Osiris	57
10	The Setereion	60
11	The Mystery Play	64
12	Journey to Fayum	95
13	The Labyrinth	98
14	Kha'emwaset	108
15	Journey to Men-nefer	115
16	The Serapeum	120
17	Journey to Saqqara	124
18	Opening of Mouth Ceremony	132
19	The Double Sphinx	140
20	Final Initiation	145
	The Heb Sed Two Festival	157
	Glossary	165

List of illustrations

Khemit	5
Aeon of Set	29
Map of Temple of Karnak and Luxor	46
Map of constellation of Ursa Major	53
Osiris & Isis	64
Horus & Set: The Great Battle	87
Sobek	99
Ptah image by Billie Walker-John	115
Khaem with Apis bull	121
A Sem Priest	125
The mysterious Tekenu	136
Opening of the mouth ceremony	137
Set: The Return	161

Introduction

I write this for my dear late friend, Billie Walker-John. She was an extra-ordinary person, whose passing in the year 2000 affected me deeply. Although originally from America, she spent the last part of her life in Gwent, South Wales, with her husband Nigel and 10 cats. Towards the end of her life she never ventured beyond the shores of Britain. When she stayed with me in London she would tell me how her spirit continuously ventured to the ancient realms of Egypt.

In 1990 Billie co-wrote *Inner Guide to Egypt* with Alan Richardson. The book was, for her, the culmination of thirty years of fascination with, and devotion to, Pharaonic Egypt. It also marked the end of her magickal apprenticeship.

Owing to the limitations she had to conform to regarding the above publication, a great deal of the work she had envisaged was left out. In order to finish off the work she started in her own short lifetime, in a sense I write this with her and, through her. The plan and the outline are both from her, as she visits seven specific centres in ancient Egypt in order to touch upon the essence of that most slandered, feared and criticized of all the gods, Set, Prince of Darkness. This is not just a journey that she always wanted to do in life, but also a piece of magick that can now be achieved after her death.

Through Billie, I will attempt to cut through so much of what we now think of as Ancient Egypt, and only the bare bones will remain. Symbolic figureheads such as Osiris and Amon will be discussed, but not elevated, and favoured centres of apparent importance or popularity will be by-passed. This will not be a book for those who wish to play tourist, dropping off here for a quick sensation, or stopping there for an imagined photo-shoot, it will be an experience for all those who wish to embrace the origin and notion of Set, and Set's values.

This poem is also written for and about Set, as a stand against such dogmatic philosophies of religious history. Protest is needed: since the middle to late kingdom this emphasis of Set and his influence has passed from historiography into our culture at large. So much of our current literature and thought rejects the role of the scapegoat in mythology, denies the importance of his individual genius in social change, refuses to recognise his superiority, and has a fear of uniqueness and discord.

In recording the mythical life of Set, we have applauded him. The strength and warmth of his intellect demand similar warmth in his dramatic performance throughout ancient Egyptian history. To adopt an attitude of detachment, particularly towards the ancient and unknown, can bar from sight those many scenes glimpsed by the historian who approaches the role of reconstructing an era with sympathy, insight and understanding. Neither the truth nor the equilibrium of scholarship is disturbed by controlled imagination and honest praise of this much-maligned Egyptian god.

The fatalistic approach that informed authoritarians have taken regarding the Set figure, has received increasingly influential support, while the various concepts of him have appeared in varied guises. It is quite apt to quote A L Kroeber's 'deep-seated, blind and intricate forces that shape culture'. The hero is a particle caught in the drift of religious and cosmic history, a mere by - product and what happened, had to happen.

We are portraying the mythological concept and personality of Set not in order to worship a hero, but to recognise him as a leader *and* a hero. Set strives to take his stand against 5,000 years of a 'drift of history' with the introduction of Osirion and Amonite tradition, and a preconditioning before being replaced by Christianity.

In this Ur-Egypt, it is the Pantheon group of Osiris, Re and all the other 'good' Gods of Egypt who are the usurpers, the intruders. It is the sovereignty of Set they seek to overthrow, not the other way around; an eldritch worship they must overturn and vanquish. This they do to become the victors, the 'Good Guys' of a sun-lit Egypt filled with their worship. The stellar darkness of the oldest Egypt is overturned, demonised and rejected - but not forgotten. The worship of Set, his liturgies and images, seep through into the religions of the solar gods - the old ways always remain in Egypt. In this regard, they act as the backdrop against which the victors develop.

It is my intent in this book to return the backdrop to its original primacy, to reveal what came before the victors, to provide the inner guide to Set. We tend today, due to our Western Judeo-Christian conditioning, to see this older Set and his landscape as stereotyped 'evil' that is always destined to be overcome by the equally stereotyped 'good'. This conditioning usually tends to narrow its focus on the viewpoint of the 'good guys', the winners. Only rarely do we consider the viewpoint of the 'bad guys', the demonised or conquered. Maybe we do not want to hear what it will tell us about ourselves. In this book we let Set figuratively speak for himself. We feel it is time to hear his side of the story. He has only had to wait 5,000 years for it to be told.

Set has become a controversial figure in recent historical researches and discussion, but all the facts are not being disclosed. Scholars have attempted to strip him of his reputation for originality and genius, harmony and pure brotherly love by maintaining that his chaotic actions universally were something to be highlighted and condemned. They have called attention to his murderous ways and continued alienation of all things harmonious.

Whoever delves into the fathomless secrets of the land of the Nile, or is held captive by the fascination of the five millennia of history before the Christian era, cannot help but admire the great kings of ancient Egypt who worshipped and fought under the name of Set and continued to bring both fame and fortune to this black land. Whatever the true judgement of Set's personality and forbearing as the first son of Nut is discussed in this poem and will help to provide a more valid interpretation of his true nature.

The Song of Meri-Khem - A Pilgrim's Journey is intended to act as a guidebook on more than one level. In material terms any intrepid traveller should be able to use this as an adjunct to the official guidebooks, and find unusual, unexpected insights into the particular places that are so relevant to the Set of myth and history. In spiritual, magickal terms, the reader who will make the quality effort needed will find his unconscious resonating to awakening energies that have been ignored too long. The illustrations, the maps and the imagery will have the effect of keys that will enable them to access and explore new realms.

We will need a map, and a simple route to take us from Nekhen to Thebes, and Naqada/ Ombos to Abydos, Fayum, and Memphis. Finally, the move will be from Saqqara to Giza, also known as Rostau. We will explore these places, while also being aware that we are following the shapes that are echoed in the asterisms, or star groups that are to be found in the constellations of Ursa Major.

I am not suggesting that the people of Khemit placed these particular sites in an order to echo a stellar configuration. However, the ancient Egyptians had stellar knowledge when they built the Pyramids that accurately aligned them towards the north, and their sides deviate from true north by less than three arc minutes, less than a twentieth of a degree. That is extremely accurate in terms of orientation.

We will look at how the seven stars within Ursa Major played their part in ancient Egypt. We know this constellation as the Plough, or the Great Bear, known to the people of Khemit as Mesxet, and was originally seen as the Thigh of the Bull. The mighty bull itself was always known as one of the sacred animals of Set. Ursa Minor whose star pattern echoes the other almost exactly, and whose tip is actually the present day Pole Star. The Egyptians associated this with the Dog of Set, the jackal god Anubis, who was the originator of embalming, his task being to glorify and preserve all the dead in order to live again. In fact we cannot really avoid them, for they are eternally above the head of every pilgrim who seeks to travel in the land of Khemit. Ursa Major also resembles the adze used for the supremely important ritual known as the Opening of the Mouth ceremony. According to those who have made an intensive study of ancient Egyptian medicine, the device was used in different ways: for opening of the trachea when someone was bitten by a snake or stung by a scorpion, or for clearing out the mouth of newborn babes, to help their breathing. But to the star watchers and stellar magickians of Egypt the important thing about the adze was that it could, magickally, bestow 'Eternal Life', as a symbol of Ursa Major and Ursa Minor that never sinks below the horizon.

Although eight places will be visited in total, these will still correspond with the constellation of Ursa Major in as much as the stars Alcor and Mizar are grouped together.

Apart from the pilgrim following this constellation route of eight places, she will also be beginning her journey at a point in Egypt called Nekhen that was the very foundation of civilisation of this land, and a personal awareness of her being. The places she chooses are not only popular ancient territories of worship of the god Set, but will also correspond to man's seven subtle bodies as the etheric is the blueprint upon which the physical is built. This includes the various systems, the nervous system, the circulatory system, the brain and the heart. The ancients considered that the organization of the universe corresponded with the structure of the human body. The universe was the 'macrocosm' and the body was the 'microcosm'. Hence the top of the head corresponded to the top of the universe, the North Star. Ascension macro-cosmically through the heavens (often numbered as seven) to the highest heaven corresponded to ascension microcosmically of the fire-snake (Kundalini), the primal source or power that usually lays dormant in the non-initiate.

Macrocosm = great world, universe

Microcosm = man viewed as the epitome of the universe in miniature

As our pilgrim honours the god Set, she must visit Naqada also known as Ombos or Nubty meaning gold. This is true Setian territory where Set was supposedly born or rather fell to earth after bursting from his starry mother's side. This particular place was a real melting pot and a crossroad where peoples from all over the known world gathered to either share new innovative ideas, or continued with their own particular primitive lifestyle. This cross-section of citizens varied not only in ethnic groupings, but also in social strata.

Thebes (Waset) will be her next destination after Naqada where she will visit the awe-inspiring monument of Karnak. This is the city of cities, a place of sunlight and shadow. The pilgrim will experience the notion of initiation as she explores the innermost depths of this great temple of hidden stairways, and underground caverns. She will be plunged into the darker side of Karnak, as she 'comes into her being'. She will also be introduced to Kha'emwaset, Sem priest to his father Rameses

II, another true Setian. He was no ordinary priest, but also Egypt's first archaeologist. Together they will explore the many sites chosen for Meri-Khem's initiation.

Sometimes the constellation of Ursa Major will take on a symbolic monumental form as she treads the age-worn paving slabs of the Temple of Luxor (Ipet-resyt), embodying the true cosmic form of the god Set, thus helping the land and the psyche of the pilgrim to resonate. She will look upon the plan of this temple as the microcosm working her way through it as we would our body.

Her journey to Abydos (Abju) will be to reveal how the introduction of Osiris into the frame is a later interpolation, and indicates how completely the Osirian cult had usurped the original state of affairs showing Osiris for what he really is.

Meri-Khem's experience in the great labyrinth at Fayum teaches her to explore all those untapped and unvisited areas of her psyche. Each part of the brain is like a room with many windows. Some people live their entire life in one room. They leave this earth plane having experienced little, and questioning nothing.

The journey to Memphis (Men-nefer) will be made by the mysterious Henu Boat, purportedly fuelled by light, perhaps an echo of solar power. It is on this boat that Kha'emwaset tells the intrigued Meri-Khem more about himself, and his duty to his father, as High Priest.

From the Temple of Ptah in Memphis Meri-Khem is taken to see the mysterious Serapeum, the final resting place of the Apis bull. In the latter part of the twentieth century a team of Japanese Egyptologists unearthed a hidden chamber. Within this chamber a golden mask was discovered and believed to be that of the famed Kha'emwaset himself, but this is only speculation.

Her next visit is to the fields of Saqqara where she will witness the ordeal Pharaoh has to endure in order to prove his strength and courage to continue his reign as king of Egypt.

In a secret location of a chosen site beneath Saqqara the pilgrim is privy to a wondrous sight, the enactment of the Opening of Mouth Ceremony that was usually carried out on the recently departed king. But in some cases a live Pharaoh was subjected to this ordeal. This is truly a Setian practice.

Finally, she will go on to experience a cognitive awakening as she travels on to her final destination, Giza, also known in ancient times as Rostau. Here she will realize her eventual 'coming into being'. This will be her ultimate goal and re-birth in the inner sanctum of the Great Pyramid of Khufu.

Chapter One
Pilgrimage

Came the pilgrim, from the Westland,
From the city of skyscrapers,
From the land of concrete jungle,
Where polluted minds of many
Search for God in Mammon daily.

She the silent, dreamy maiden,
She the wilful and the wayward,
Was the bravest of her sisters,
Discontented with her mean lot.
'I have no interest in saints and martyrs,
Or your chosen, or your virgins,
Keep your grails and Templar mysteries,
And redemptive sacrifices.

'I need to know about the stellar,
About the temples and their mysteries,
Lead me to the ancient star gods,
And the ancient tribes who followed.'

So the pilgrim journeyed eastward,
Left the city far behind her,
Left the polluted minds of many,
For the kingdom of the East-wind.
O'er dry land, and the ocean,

Many days she travelled eastward,
On a boat sea-bound for Egypt,
To the first land of the Pharaohs,
Steeped in mystery, of the first time,
Of the first god, of the star child,
That walked the black land
By the old Nile.

Along a river, winding, snake-like,
Among the green reeds, and the rushes,
From the delta and the desert,
Comes the pilgrim, the question maker,
'Who was Sut-Typhon?
Who was Sutekh?'

'Tell me of this fallen star god,
Tell me of the shrines and temples,
Tell me of the hallowed places,
Lead me to them,
Let me worship,
In the great halls to this dog god,
Let me commence initiation,
Let my name be, Meri-Khem.'

Chapter Two
Journey to Nekhen

South of Esna, to Kom el-Ahmar,
She did travel, she did journey,
To find answers to her questions,
Whence these legends and traditions.

Finds the ancient Iri-Nekhen,
First cult centre, to the god Set,
Also, City of the Falcon,
Twin brother of god Sutekh,
First town in Upper Khemit,
Alkaid in Ursa Major
And lowest centre of the body.

Dynastic Khem began in Nekhen,
Power centre to hunter-gatherer,
Joined by farmers and the herders,
Final days of nomad wanderer,
Joined a vibrant busy city,

And beside them sang the singer,
Sang of wondrous birth and being,
Songs of ancient lore and wisdom,
So the pilgrim sat and listened
To the wondrous story-teller.

In Nekhen they built a temple,
A shrine of mud, wood and wicker,
In the rear an oval courtyard,
Of brush and reeds for boundary,
Between the sacred, and blasphemous,
Symbolised earth, man and cosmos.

In this open oval courtyard,
Flanked by many coloured banners,
Stood Nekheb, vulture goddess,
Keeper of the city Nekhen.

Overlooking the central dais,
Seated were the great and royal,
Early kings of Upper Egypt,
Witnessed daily animal slaught'ring,
Fanned by pungent kyphi incense,
Masking senses, freeing spirits,
Typhonic creatures, Setian symbols,
Grinding off'rings over black soil.

Came the shaman dressed for ritual,
With his wand and skin of a leopard,
Skin that was the mark of Nu'it,
Bears the stars of night upon it,
Within each star is held a Neter,
That works the magick of the dark side.

Then the shaman sang the first note,

Song of Merikhem

Sang to them with voice majestic,
Like the sound of far-off echoes,
Falling into deepest chasms,
Listen to the words of wisdom,
Listen to the words of dawning,
From the past ancestor memory.

So the early priests of Khemit
Controlled the masses with their magick,
Kept the soul and country thriving.
Great was the Setian shaman,
Great was ancient Iri-Nekhen.
Meri-Khem sat musing, dreaming,
Sees the first king known as Narmer,
Scorpion Pharaoh great in bearing,
Who brought together warring brothers.

Set and Horus face each other,
Wearing double crowns of Khemit,
White and Red of Heru-Sutekh,
Symbolised the states of Khemit.

Twinning Powers are arisen,
Divisions of the nature spirit,
Between the higher self and lower,
Between right brain and the left,
Between the anima and the animus,
Between the female and the male,
Of many binaries unending.

Of the moments of uniting,
Of the very first co-joining,
Of these sacred twins undying,
Set and Horus stand for justice,
Establish laws and truth eternal,
Across the delta and the deserts,
Of the great expanse of Khemit.

Chapter Three
Journey to Naqada

Watched by Alcor in Ursa Major,
Over Khem the Star of Evening,
Bless'ed Nu'it shining splendid,
Hangs suspended in the starlight,
All the cosmos flushed with purple.

Then the sky was stained with crimson,
With her blood the stars are reddened,
Primeval goddess, stellar mother,
Bringing onward seven star souls,
Birthing forth her star-child Sutekh.

Cried the star one to her baby,
'O my son, my true beloved!
Son of Evening, God of Dawning!'
Thus did come the child of wonder,
First male Neter, Great Lord Sutekh!

Hail Great Nu'it and her first-born,
First born Neter of the black-land.

Diving down beneath the stardust,
Passing silent through the twilight,
From the astral to Terra Firma,
Drops to Nubty, now Naqada,

Son of Evening Star descended,
Son of tenderness and passion,
Filled with fire in his bosom,
Filled with beauty in his spirit.

See the mystery of his being,
Hear the splendour in his speaking,
In his mouth the words are melting,
From his lips the songs are forming,
Songs echoed from distant ages,
Music from the stellar waters,
Music from the whole creation.

Golden child and dearest Sutekh,
Gave to Nubty precious gold ore,
Gold was holy gold was fertile,
Gold of kingship, gold of Ombos,
Torn from darkness like the star child,
From darkness of the earth world,
All the mines, a gift from this one.

All were joyous in Naqada,
Claimed was Sutekh as their great one,
Claimed was he their greatest offspring,
Guardian to Peribsen the royal
Who built the many temples to him.
Set is great! Set is master!
Let us honour him in splendour,
Let us gather b'neath these rafters,

Aeon of Set

In his shrine renowned and ancient,
Let us sing the song of Sutekh,
Burn the sweet incense of kyphi,
Make libations to the star god,
Make libations of beer from barley,
Of the barley from the earth god.

From the far outstretching spaces,
Long-haired raiders came from Sumer,
Came in high-prowed ships to conquer
The simple folk of old Naqada,
Smashing them with pear-shaped maces,
Made of dark blue stone of lapis.

From these people, folk of Sumer,
Sprang the sacred kings who conquered,
Iry-Pat was their grand name,
Members of a special blood-clan.

Distant were these ancient regents,
Tracing back to distant watchers,
Echoed through the land of Khemit,
Elite and great these founding families,
A ruling class that founded kingship,
Made their kingdom in the valley.
Thus did Narmer dig a channel,
Dug a ditch that crossed the desert,
Crossed the wilderness and wasteland,
Filled with waters from the Nile god,

Song of Merikhem

Pushing back the sands of Khemit,
Springs to life the land of Egypt.

Grassy hills replace the sand dunes,
Fields and forests now created,
Old life gives way to rich and plenty,
All the peoples sang together,
'We are one! We are a nation!
May all our kings be known as Horus!
May their names live on forever!

'Let us unite the twins of Nu'it,
Let us call them Sutekh-Heru,
Form Two Lands of ancient Khemit.'

Thus Meri-Khem the pilgrim waited,
Patiently she sat and listened,
Cried her in a voice of wonder,
'Show me Nut, I pray thee, show me,
Guide me Set, I pray thee, guide me.

'On this land I walk, I wander,
Search the great expanse of heaven,
Not to see the moon at evening,
Or to see the golden sunlight,
But to see the Bear in heaven,
To see the stars of Sutekh's body,
Feel the power of his mighty,
To the threshold of his being,

That I may rest within his dwelling,
In this wondrous stellar kingdom,
And travel on the astral level.'

Chapter Four
Journey to Thebes (Waset)

On to Waset Meri travelled,
To the hundred-gated city,
Karnak! greatest temple city ever,
Built by Antef, ancient warlord.
First he made a lodge for praying,
Seven days and nights he dwelt there,
He had dreams and visions many,
Of an ancient hidden old one.

'Who art thou who hides in shadows?'
There came a voice within the shadows,
'I am Amon, god of Waset,'
Spake the voice within the shadows.
'Where is your temple god of Waset?'
'You will build my house of worship,
But I must always be hidden,
In a golden shrine you'll keep me,
Bathe and dress me in the morning
And sing a song at dusk of evening.'

So Antef carried out his orders
Built a glorious temple for him
Made of finest reddest granite.

As he promised, Antef placed him

In the darkest corner of the temple,
Made a shrine of gold around him.

'I am pleased with you now Antef.
Leave me now, but keep me hidden!'

All rejoiced in Karnak Temple,
Sang songs of praise up to their warlord.
'Antef! Great lord of our nation!
Crown him Pharaoh of all Khemit.'
Shifted power and the magick
From old Nekhen up to Waset.

Several Antefs and Mentu-hoteps
Graced the throne of Karnak Temple,
Sem Priest now replaced the shaman,
Gave new power to their sceptres,
Fashioned after Sutekh's image.

A wand to soak telluric currents,
Thus they felt it rising, rising,
Like the djinns of ancient past days.
Felt the forces spiral upwards,
Felt the pulsing through their bare feet.

Channelled were these potent currents,
That founded ancient power centres,
That founded ancient Karnak Temple,
Amon once a local godling

Song of Merikhem

Now the greatest god in Karnak.
Chose fair Mut as consort goddess,
Gave birth to Khonsu gentle moon child.
So was formed the Karnak triad.

Within the walls of Amon's temple,
Are the many secret pass-ways.
Many are the hidden hallways,
Leading to the rooms of mystery,
Rooms of old initiation.

Chapter Five
Journey to Karnak

On a moonlit night in Nesut-Towi,
Meri-Khem did choose to wander,
Down the sacred steps of sandstone,
Past the avenue of Sphinxes,
With heads of Amon, ancient Ram God,
Age of Aries in its prime time.

Onward through the Hypostyle Hall,
Pillars like forests crowd around her,
Onward to the shrine of Amon,
A dim light burning in his sanctum,
Just a flame of one who's hidden.

He is locked within his sanctum,
Then in morning time is opened,
Floods of light fall on his body,
He is washed and perfumed daily,
Dressed and fed alone by Pharaoh.

Incense burnt in copper vessels,
Many prayers are uttered to him,
Amon is left again to slumber.

Chapter Six
Journey to the Temple of Khonsu

Now she ventures to the waters,
Of the sacred lake of deity,
Mists are swirling 'cross this water,
Bathed is she within the vapours,
Cleansing mind and soul and body,
All the unseen spirits see her,
Then the ancient voices call her.

'Meri you must keep on walking.
Through the vastness of this temple,
Across the great expanse of paving,
To the south-west place of worship,
To the moon child's inner sanctum,
Through the portals of his temple.'

Watched by many older idols,
Etched on walls of yellow sandstone,
Walking onwards, crossing hallways,
Reached the limits of the vestry.

She is cloaked in outer darkness,
Feels her inner heart beat thudding.
Internal voices asking questions,

Whispering phantoms from the shadows,
All wanting answers to her reasons
For her entry to this sanctum.
Meri-Khem then makes to answer.

'I am Meri-Khem the pilgrim,
Seeking mystery of past ages,
Seeking my initiation.'

From the shadows tall and regal,
Kha'emwaset walks toward her,
He, the Mightiest of Magickians,
He, the mightiest among the many.

In the faint light of the sconces,
Gleams his well-oiled golden body,
Grasping firmly in his right hand,
Holds Uwas sceptre of Lord Sutekh.

Kha'em's clothed in finest linen,
Clothed is he in richest garments
Hanging over his broad shoulders,
He wears the fur-skin of the leopard,
Worn only by the rank of Sem Priest,
Order of the great god Sutekh.

With these words he utters to her,
'I will be your guide from now on,
I shall guide you and shall teach you,

Song of Merikhem

I will teach you ancient by-laws,
I am lord of inner levels,
Lord of Nature, Light and Darkness,
Of the sacred mystery schooling.'

She did pass and cross the threshold,
To the inner shrine of Khonsu.
Centred in this room of granite,
Stands the altar stark and empty,
Stands before it is the pilgrim,
Meri-Khem in her beginning.

Kha'emwaset takes her two hands,
Placing them upon the altar,
Energy pulses through her body,
Light turns into velvet darkness,
Dawns the mystery in her being.

Then he urges her to take steps,
And with darkness cloaked and guarded,
Unashamed and unaffrighted,
Walks around the granite altar,
Walks the sacred, magick circle.

Sevenfold around the altar,
Anti-clockwise she does walk on,
Counts the footsteps round the flagstones.
Ancient flagstones worn in memory,
Memory of the other pilgrims,

Who sought to travel this same journey,
To receive initiation,
Of the lower mental plane.

Now she pauses, taking deep breaths,
Breathes in tempo to a drum beat.

Like a mantra, swirl the sound waves,
Holds the pilgrim, the question maker,
In this trance state she is guided,
By the Sem Priest Kha'emwaset.

Hears his voice say in the darkness,
Hears his voice as sweet as honey,
'Life in death, I will protect you.
Look upon the granite altar,
Press the pictogram down firmly.'

Rose a sound of granite sliding,
Rose a great door on the far wall,
Through a secret sandstone portal,
Leading downward into darkness,
Are the many steps of doubting,
Melancholy is the pilgrim,
Sadness in her core of being,
She is leaving her old values,
Being stripped of worn-out standards,
Watching outer shell dissolving.

Song of Merikhem

'Is this the price of my beginning?'
Corridors of darkness greet her,
Pungent incense wafts around her,
Stinging nostrils, eyes and throat-way,
In the murky swirl she listens,
To the sounds of distant footsteps,
Walking forward? Walking backwards?

Now confusion's her companion,
To bewitch her in its power,
Now she hears the voices screaming,
'We'll drive you back with much dishonour,
To your land of greed and plenty!'

Crypt and cavern beckon to her,
Seven cells along this hallway,
Womb-like are they in construction,
Labyrinths of much confusion,
Cloaked in mystery, cloaked in magick.
Each one Meri enters deftly, surely,
'This is where all things did springeth!
Like a coiling spring unwinding
Helps to loosen sacred psyche,
Awakening my pineal memory,
Nurturing my sleeping reason,
Just through darkness can this happen,
Of the secret Rites of Mystery,
Practiced in the ancient caverns,
In the subterranean chambers,

Under shrines and out of limits.'

Now she drifts within a vacuum,
Around her swirls a different ether
Sounds like voices from afar off,
Now wildly in the air around her,
Cold and eerie, screaming laughing,
Sound of wings and feathers flapping
'I will not listen!' cries the pilgrim,
'I will go and face my demons,
Prove my worth to all the priesthood.'

From the empty air appearing,
Comes in silence like a phantom.

'I am Shu, lord of this kingdom!'

Now his forces whip around her,
Sucking out the old and dated,
Airing senses, breathing new life,
Sylphs that prey upon her being,
Feather-light she drifts in currents,
Wisp and cloud-like is her body.

'May this bliss be never-ending.'
Now she sees a different phantom,
Sekhmet-Montu now surrounds her
With his hot and shining tresses.
Fires stream out from his body,

SONG OF MERIKHEM

From his nostrils, sparks are shooting,
Licking round her airy body,
Firing senses, firing new life,
Weaving webs of golden fire,
Weaving webs of wondrous splendour,
Salamanders whip about her,
Till in flame they burst and sparkle,
Cloaking her in glorious fire-light.

From the solitude of ether,
And the fire-encircled bindings,
She is plunged into the waters,
Whips the waters all around her,
Quenching flames of Sekhmet-Montu.

To and fro is tossed the pilgrim,
Play the forces of the Undine,
Over-burdened now the pilgrim,
Frightened by the airy creatures,
Singed and burnt by salamanders,
Now plunged into blue-black water.

She swims the deep in all directions,
Dark below her flowed like Hapuy,
With fingers flowing like the waters,
Grabs the pilgrim by her tresses.

As the pilgrim swims and struggles,
Rises gasping to the surface,

To the vault of Terra Firma,
To the old realm of the Apis,
There the level banks have risen,
To the mound of Ben-en-et,
Above the first primeval ocean,
Where first emerged the ancient Earth God.
To the Opet, House of Horus.

'Through the elemental stages,
Once unborn to live and flourish,
From the spaces wrapped in shadows,
Cleansed by Sutekh in true darkness,
Where so many priests have perished,
I have surfaced I have triumphed!
This, my first initiation.'

Bathed in golden light of Heru,
Leaves the Opet temple, happy,
As a dweller on the threshold,
On the dawning of her first day
Eyes wide-open ventures forward.

North, east then south she strides on,
Skirts the Karnak Temple proper,
Returns again to her first dawning,
At the breaking of the first-light,
At the early hour of morning,
Straightway then she hastens southwards,
By a road-way lined with Sphinxes,
Walks the road to Ipet-resyt.

Chapter Seven
Journey to the Temple of Luxor

Beating is the sun at noonday,
Weary is she by her ordeal,
Sits beside a Sphinx and watches,
On the roadway waits and listens,
For Kha'emwaset her protector,
Waits an age for this magickian,
She now dozes by the roadside,
Fills the air with dreamy colour.

Finally the priest returneth,
Kha'emwaset of Men-nefer,
Fixed his gaze upon the South-east
Toward the great and perfect temple,
Created in lord Sutekh's image,
Embodiment of Ursa Major,
Mesxet of ancient Khemit.

Together now they venture southwards,
Along the avenue of Sphinxes.

Now the darkness fills the night sky,
The stars of Nut come out to greet them,
As they enter Sutekh's kingdom.

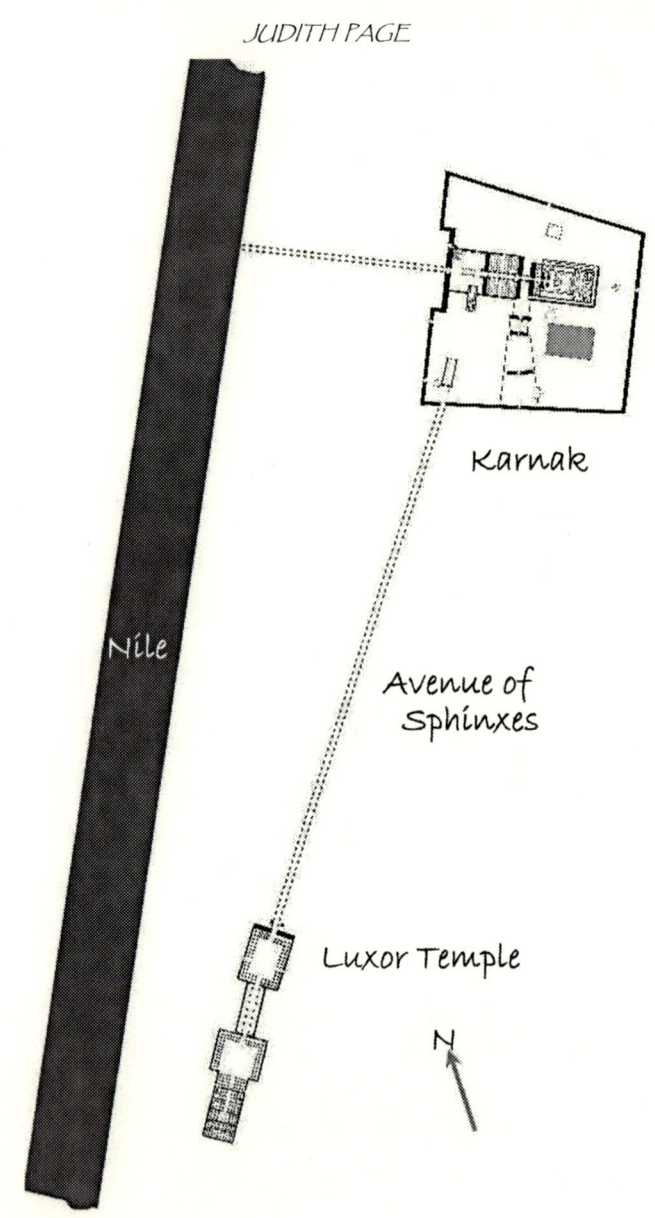

Map of Temple of Karnak and Luxor

Song of Merikhem

'Meri look now above you,
At the stars that shine upon you,
Great is this Bear in the heavens,
Great is the plough in this region,
Megrez, Phad, Merak and Dubhe,
Boundary stars of Karnak Temple.

'All is clear as I gaze upwards,
I have walked the stellar pathway,
On the land of this great temple,
The microcosm on the earth plane.'

Looms before her, rising upwards,
Two obelisks, born of granite,
Pharaoh's votive to all deity,
Rooting earth and piercing skyward,
Joining earth up to the heavens.

Meri stands before the portal,
Shifts her gaze to mammoth figures,
Kha'emwaset points out proudly,
'These are of my father Rameses.

'Ipet-resyt awaits your entry.'
Designed and built by Amon-hotep,
Added to by many Pharaohs,
Masterpiece of Setian current,
Shaped and fashioned using numbers,
Through geometric, and the symbol.

Pure forms of man's connection,
With the macrocosm way above.

Meri feels this Setian current
Through the structure thus divided
Into seven equal chambers
In the shape of Ursa Major.
Hears the voices to the old gods,
Sounds of music, words of wonder,
Beckon her to follow Kha'em
Who now enters as the Sem Priest,
Walks toward the sacred sanctum,
Total centre of man's being.

From the farthest realms of morning,
Comes the Lector priest to greet him,
He the priest of prayer and cleansing,
Prepares and makes the Sem Priest pure.
Washing mouth and face with natron,
Priest and Prince approach the sanctum,
Followed by the pilgrim Meri.

Come the sweetest temple singers,
Shaking sistra gently swaying,
Singing notes so warm and welcome,
That awake Amon from slumber.

Kha'emwaset lay prostrated,
Rose and bowed before the doorway

Song of Merikhem

Of the sanctum of great Amon,
Broke the red clay seal before he entered.

All was dark within the sanctum,
Lamps were lit beside the statue
Beside the great and golden Amon.
Censors filled the shrine with fragrance,
All inhale the fumes of khyphi
That waft freely around the temple
Breathing life into the statue
Bringing life to great god Amon.
Taking up some mist fine linen,
Dipped and soaked in scented water,
Kha'em touched his perfect body,
Washed him slowly and in silence,
Fed him fine foods with much reverence.

Clothed him once again in raiment
Of freshest purest whitest linen.

Kha'em steps away from Amon,
Raises both hands upward, slowly
Utters up a prayer to Amon.

'O mighty force of earth and heaven
That quickened waters of all chaos,
Breathe sacred life here unto Amon.
O mighty power of earth and heaven
The Great Spirit, Divine Creator,

Impart to me your words of wisdom
So I may once again be mighty.
O Great Cackler, O great Amon
Who sprang forth from times primeval
As an egg, Akasha symbol,
Made all things come into being,
Spread your bounty over Waset.'

Meri stood in awesome silence
Watching Kha'em in devotion.

After several more libations
Kha'emwaset left the sanctum,
Closed and sealed the door in silence.
Then he broke the silence saying,
'Here we celebrate the Opet
Where god and goddess meet together.

'My father Pharaoh makes his tribute,
Gives the bread out to the masses,
Distributes beer made out of barley.

'All my family gather round him,
Worship Pharaoh as a deity.
Then there is a grand procession
Along the avenue of Sphinxes,
To the waters of the river.'
On a barge that sailed from Beh-det
Awaits Heru for his consort,

Song of Merikhem

Hat-hur, in her golden splendour
Arrives from Iunet, north of Waset,
Greets his long awaited consort.

All along the Nile are floating
Many barges decked with flowers,
Singers, dancers, soldiers, nobles
Gather there to watch and marvel.
Meanwhile in the temple proper
Priest and Pharaoh pray together,
Holy rituals are enacted.
'There my father's soul, his great Ka,
Merge and transform his pure being,
Deity enters Pharaoh's body,
It is a wondrous transformation.'
In great numbers crowds now gather
Watching Pharaoh's re-emergence,
No longer Pharaoh but immortal
As King and god are joined together.

Meri stood there, watching, waiting,
Looked with two eyes of wonder,
Eyes that always seemed to question.

'Let us walk now through the temple
That is the structure of our body.
Divine is this temple structure,
Feel the surging of the power!'
Cried Meri-Khem the pilgrim,
'Is it power? Or just enchantment!

I do feel different in my body,
But my heart is sad within me,
I have longings, yearnings, strivings,
I feel alone within this temple.'

Kha'em touched her gently saying,
'We have put you to the trial,
It is the re-tune of your body.
The sacred number of all being
Has entered once again your body,
We shall leave this place together.'

With her guide and her companion
Meri left the sacred temple.
Took with her ancient star-lore
From the body of great Nu'it,
And made her way to ancient Abju.

SONG OF MERIKHEM

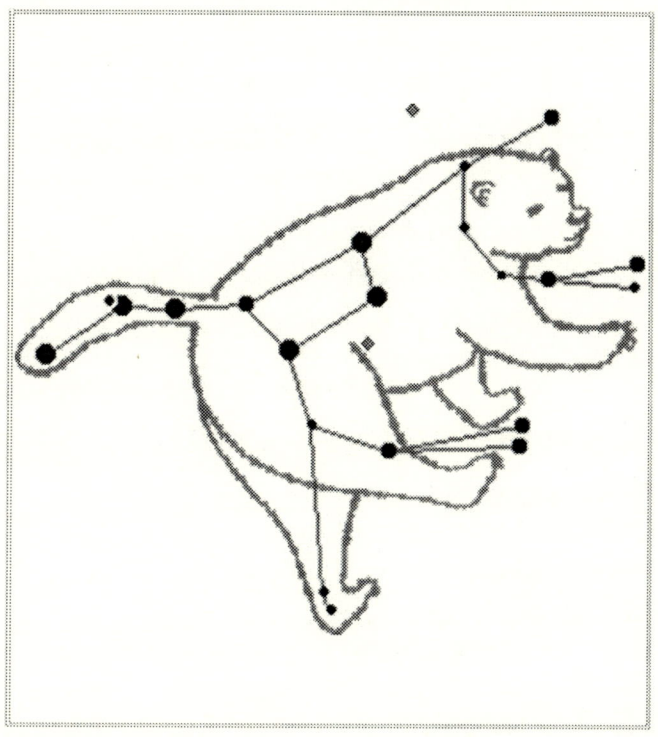

Map of constellation of Ursa Major

Chapter Eight
Journey to Abydos (Abju)

On the long and distant journey
To the portals of the north-star,
Kha'em told a tale to Meri
Of the early god of Abju.

'He was known as Khenta-ment-hes,
From the dog group of Candides,
Of his many ancient old names,
Anubis of the Khemit White Land,
Desert region of lord Sutekh,
Protector of this resting place.

'The Kingly built a temple to him,
A shrine of mud, reeds and wicker,
Sacrificed the animals many,
In the name Khenta-ment-hes.

' Thus he held supreme dominion
And hereafter and forever
Over all the winds of heaven!
Till the sun and moon changed places.

' And the Night-sun setting eastward,
Till the sky was red with sunrise,
Till the pallid moon, the Night-sun,

Song of Merikhem

Rose above the sombre Abju.

'In the desert outside Abju,
Mourners left libation vessels,
To honour passing of their loved ones,
In protection of the dog-god.'

So they walked the land together
To the resting place of thousands,
All around the earth was reddened
With the many earth fired vessels.

Meri-Khem stooped down and gathered
Two tiny cups of ancient giving,
Gestured with two hands uplifted,
Sent a joyous prayer to heaven,
Within her felt both joy and sadness,
Felt a tingling in her fingers,
Sensed a knowing in her being,
Dropped the tiny clay pots earthward
Into the soft white sand of Abju.

Chapter Nine
The Rise of Osiris

'Came a day when all did change here,
From the far east-land of Sumer,
Came a god to ancient Khemit,
Name of Enki of Eri-du,
Perhaps he was an ancient chieftain,
And was raised in adoration.

'But he of many-sided natures,
Imposed his will on sacred Abju,
This Wasir, this Osiris,
Took to dwelling 'neath the surface
God of life and much abundance,
Makes the corn and barley sprout forth,
Makes the beer from golden barley,
Makes all men to sing his praises.
Unlike other eastern nations,
Was the male god of the earth-land,
Such a puzzle, this Osiris.

'As he lay down on his broad back,
Many green herbs sprouting from him,
Could this also be more borrowing?
From the ancient god Andjeti,
Who hailed from Djedu in the delta,
Where all is green and plants a'plenty,

Song of Merikhem

Thus is named, Andjeti waters.

' So Osiris claiming Abju
Crook and flail he carries proudly,
Mummy-dressed like Udi-mu,
On his head a crown with feathers,
Beautiful white crown called the Antef.'

Then asked Meri-Khem the pilgrim,
'What did happen to Khenta-menthes?'

Kha'em not at ease with Wasir,
Took deep breaths then finally answered,
'He thrust aside the ancient dog-god,
And spread the word of true salvation.

'But he needed a new consort
To fill the gap of this staged mystery,
Hence was found the Libyan Isa,
Goddess of a Western province.
'Not content with this new image,
Rewrote the myth of goddess Nu'it,
Of the great unmated mother.
Created then gods Shu and Tefnut,
Twin lions that govern east and west,
Who gave birth to Geb and Nu'it,
Brother and sister in the cosmos,
They had children five in number.
Asar, Heru, Set and Isa,

Nephthi was the last to follow.
Five extra days were gained in number,
Added to the lunar calendar.'

Pharaoh Sety found a temple
Built in ancient times to Sutekh.
For many days and nights he prayed there,
'Let me resurrect his temple
Make him great again in Khemit.'

Heard a voice call in the darkness,
'I hear your words to me O Sety
You shall gain what you have prayed for
But build a temple to all deity.
Hide me underneath this temple!'

Sety came forth from this dark place,
From his eyes the tears were flowing,
Bright above him shone the Great Ra,
Level spread the ground before him.

'I will build a temple splendid,
To all the gods of ancient Khemit,
They will have a place of sanct'ry,
But sealed within this hallowed sanctum,
Forever rests the shrine to Sutekh.
I will seal the doorway solid,
Only Wep-wa-wet will guard him.
For I am true to thee O Sutekh!'

Chapter Ten
The Setereion

In the dark and torn heart places,
Far beneath the sands of Abju
Is the sacred place to Sutekh.
Level spread Abju before you.
On a much higher level,
Survive in memory, in the back brain,
In our psyche we re-member.

Leaving temple for the desert,
Go the Sem Priest and the pilgrim,
They seek out a hidden entrance,
Buried deep beyond the temple,
Far below the main earth level.

Along a subterranean passage
Here they find a mystery sanctum,
It is made of greyest granite,
Cut and hewn with much precision,

In the same style as the temples,
On the plateau of ancient Rostau,
But this much older structure,
Gives no clue who really built it.

Down a central aisle they process,

Fourteen rooms surround an island,
Water channels feed the complex.

As they cross the central causeway,
Velvet blackness swirls around them,
In this odd and eerie temple,
Initiated sought their lessons,
Received instruction to the mysteries,
Made a secret pledge to Sutekh.

As they made their pledges to him,
Lay their naked hearts together,
With their naked hearts before them,
Made their promise to the future.

Sutekh turned and saw the pilgrim,
Cowering meekly in the shadows.

'This is no mortuary temple,
To a god of pure stasis,
This is but a place of chaos,
This is my sanctuary to confusion,
In the centre of this island,
Is an altar of pure granite,
Here upon the stone I lay thee.

'See the stars rise from the water,
See the reeling stars above you,
May Mesxet descend upon you,

Song of Merikhem

As the terra meets the stellar,
On the morrow and the next night,
When my mother greets her soul child,
Like a red and burning Nova,
From the heartland of my kingdom,
Reach your higher mental level.'

Tall and beautiful he stood there,
In his robes of black and golden,
'O Meri-Khem' he thus whispered,
'Bravely have you sought to find me,
But your test is not in Abju,
You must venture further northward,
Seek always a star to guide you,
I'll be with you and the Sem Priest.'

As she lay there in the darkness,
Water lapping round the edges,
Felt the thudding in her eardrums,
All around was total stillness,
All alone upon this island,
Nowhere was the sacred priesthood,
Gone was Set, no longer present,
Thus he vanished, and was seen not.
Did she dream this past encounter?

She had seen the inner sanctum,
Revealed her soul unto the Great One,
Sutekh saw the fragile earthling,

Took her to the heights of stellar,
Promised to be with her always.

From the crypt, went forth in silence,
Calling Kha'em through the darkness,
He then touches her left shoulder,
Telling her 'I am with you.'
She had shared her soul's pure secrets,
Set reached through her mortal body,
And her bursting heart within her,
Shook and trembled stars in heaven.

She still heard his voice within her,
'But tomorrow, when the sun sets
I will come again and try you.'

Sitting down, still and speechless,
At the feet of Kha'emwaset,
Seven days and nights they sat there,
In the desert by this temple,
Looked upon the splendid sunrise,
And the many varied sunsets,
Moving through the purple twilight,
Feasting on the stellar magick,
As the Great Bear swung above them,
Putting Set on high forever.

Chapter Eleven
The Mystery Play

On a balmy night in Abju,
Sits the pilgrim and Kha'emwaset,
Turned their eyes upon the sunset,
Gazed upon his father's temple,
Re-built by Sety to his soul god,
From an even older past time,
They will hear a tale of falsehood,
Shaped religion of the nations,
That will echo through the ages.

In the season of the Akhet,
In the sacred month of Khoiak,
Enacted in Great Sety's temple,
Is the mystery play of Wasir,
Many guests attended nightly,
Clothed in all their richest raiment,
Robes of linen and golden collars,
Splendid in their wigs of oiled hair,
Beautiful with beads and tassels.

So the noble guests assembled,
Courtiers, visitors and the priestly,
All are kneeling in obeisance,
As Rameses second processes forward.

Osiris & Isis

Song of Merikhem

Great excitement filled the temple,
Whilst the masses outside gathered ,
Hearing second hand proceedings,
By the criers paid by Pharaoh.

In the temple all are present,
While flowery speeches are delivered,
By the many varied Preachers,
Many blessings conferred upon them,
By the high and noble Sem Priest.

Behind the scenes the actors gather,
Checking costumes, checking make-up,
Soothing tempers, quelling stage fright,
Now dim the torches at a signal.

Then a hush spread o'er the temple,
As the linen curtain rises,
On a clear blue Nile-scape vista,
Date palms sway through airy currents
While birds fly round a dim-lit temple.

Flares and torches burn with brilliance,
Cast eerie smoke-clouds far above them,
To far-off lands where only gods live.
Thus begins the Mystery Pageant
To a fanfare rams' horns sound out.

A lonely actor enters left stage,

'Whilst I walked in golden sunshine,
Young, filled with youthful vigour,
Sat he amongst the reeds and rushes,
First did not hear the fatal music,
Did not hear the sound of harp-strings.
I feared not his deadly presence.

'I in full-bloom of my manhood,
Dreaming of my true beloved,
Music of surpassing beauty,
Reached my ears, and gave me pleasure,
I sought to find this sweet performer,
Did not know he was the reaper,
That he played his harp to summon,
That he searched for me alone.'

A pale blue light is then projected,
Makes the audience sit and shudder,
Then the actor speaks on sadly,
'In skeletal arms he seized me,
And bore me up unto the Atum
To become a white light being.
Far below my truelove wept on,
Whilst I floated just above her.'

Not a sound stirs in the temple,
As the actor tells his ballad,
'Death then took me to a high place,
Down below the world was spinning,

Song of Merikhem

'Like a shining shield from heaven.
In the vastness of the blue skies,
I saw strange men and stranger creatures,
From the times that are forgotten,
Like a river in reversal,
Before my eyes, time ran backwards.
I saw all men from birth to passing,
For a million years I watched them,
Life and death to time eternal,
Time becomes more isolated,
Human beings existing no more,
Men no more upon the earth plane,
Upon the earth just gods existed,
Yet still flowed the river backwards,
Beyond the time of gods to old Nun.

'Into darkness and primal chaos,
The mighty river ceased its flowing,
And so reversed this timeless river,
I watched the passion of the old gods.'
The audience sits there in amazement
As the Mystery Play continues,

'From the darkness and the chaos,
From the timelessness of old Nun,
Rose the Atum, the self-created.

'By a stroking of his member,
Mighty waves of fluids flow forth,

Silver streams of milky stardust,
Flowing 'cross the deepest dark void,
Generates twins Geb and Nu'it,
Earth and heaven thus conjoin'ed.
From this ever fateful union,
Sang of wondrous birth and being,
Of the gods Wasir and Sutekh,
Followed by Nephthys and Isa,
Finally, Haroerus joined them.

'So was first made known to mortals,
Of the first gods on this earth plane.'

Stepping back into the shadows,
The actor leaves with measured silence.

Gliding forward like a phantom,
Stands the wondrous god Osiris,
Clothed in finest, whitest linen,
Wears the crown of Upper Khemit,
Holds the crook, flail and sceptre.
A cry wells up within the temple,
As this divine god stood before them.
Pharaoh raised a hand in silence,
Thus the god Osiris speaketh:
'Behold At' Ur the mighty river!'
'Bak-her, Bak-her!' cried the Pharaoh,
'Bak-her' all repeated after Pharaoh.

SONG OF MERIKHEM

Cries Osiris, 'Behold the waters,
Swollen thus by inundation,
Behold again as they are falling,
Now behold the birds and insects.'

Butterflies glide within the temple,
Birds swoop down around the pillars,
A multi-coloured long-billed hoopoe
Settles on the crown of Rameses.

'An omen, blessings!' cry the priesthood,
'Long may Pharaoh live forever!'
Across the stage Osiris wanders,
Through the paradise he's fashioned,
But the mood is set for drama.
Set his wicked brother enters,
Blood-chilling cries are now erupting,
From the Pharaoh and the viewers.

'What have you done?' cries Set the jealous,
'Do you place yourself above me?
Am I not of equal status?
This is not your creation!
Will you not share this prize with no-one?'

The audacious, overbearing,
Spineless, older other brother
Answers with a haughty coolness,
'Our father gave it to us both now,

A right to choose how we divide it,
A pledge for good, not for evil.'

All the viewers sit in rapture,
As the words are thus embodied,
Words that ring around the pillars,
And the audience hang upon them.

As Osiris speaks thus to his brother,
Gloats upon his sibling's fury.
Gods alone know what is coming,
Osiris draws to close his speaking.

'This is the world I am revealing,
All our land in peace awaits you,
All the gates stand open for you,
To welcome you Set, my brother,
But, if you come in warlike vengeance,
And you come in rage and hatred,
Then I order you to go now,
I am weary of your quarrels,
Weary of your thirst for bloodshed,
Weary of your threats for vengeance.'

Heartless, haughty god Osiris,
Lifts his right hand in posing gesture,
Dismissing Set his troubled brother,
Dismisses him to leave his garden.

SONG OF MERIKHEM

Set draws up his massive shoulders,
Like 'bull of his mother' bellows loudly,
Screaming screeching at Osiris
'It is not well with us, O brother,
I have listened to your verbiage,
I have heard your words of stasis.'

Lifting high his golden broad-sword,
Rushes headlong t'wards Osiris,
'Long have I been waiting for you!'

Still with his right hand extended,
Mighty does the blade cut through it,
Severs hand from wrist completely.
Osiris stands there in amazement,
The viewers sit in measured silence,
Thinking this a trick of acting
Or a trick of clever lighting?

Now his hand falls downwards, slowly,
Osiris reeling back and screaming!
Clutching handless stump in anguish.
His linen white robe now staining,
With his blood the threads are reddened!

Not until the blood comes spurting,
Does the company feel uneasy,
High-pitched screams in mortal agony,
Filling all the air with terror,

Breaks the mood of these spectators,
As they witness pure carnage,
Still they sit in silent horror,
Then Osiris reached the stage edge.

Set is right up there behind him,
Grabs his stump now as a handle,
Drags his brother to the centre,
Throws him full-length sprawling forward
Where he lay there on the flag-stones,
In the crimson of his life-blood.
As Set stands in all his splendour,
In his garments red and yellow,
'O please spare me!' shrieks Osiris,
Laughing, tosses his red tresses,
Speaking ever-sweet and child-like:
'Now you fear me gentle brother,
As you lie down, pleading, writhing.'

Set now shakes with savage laughter,
That awakes the trance-like watchers,
As the play becomes more brutal,
Women scream, roar men with fury,
As they witness their god's murder.

'Spare Osiris!' all howled loudly,
But all remained there in their seating,

No spectators rise to aid him,

SONG OF MERIKHEM

Many whispered, many saying:
'We know the passions of the old gods,
Who are we but mere mortals?'

With his one remaining good hand,
Osiris reaches out at Sutekh,
'Spare me brother, I beg thee, spare me!'
Set inspecting Wasir's left arm
Inspecting it just like a butcher.

'Cut it off!' screams a mad voice,
Stirs the blood-lust of the many,
The mood now swings in opposition,
Set is stirring souls to passion,
He now moulds them all to hatred,
'Kill him, kill him!' screams another,
All sit alert to look and listen.

On her seat still sits the pilgrim,
Sits unspeaking to the Sem Priest.

Set raised up his gold sword deftly,
With a casual sweeping forward,
Now hacks off his brother's left arm,
Holds his left arm lively twitching.

At Set's feet now falls his brother,
Falls, and cannot rise from weakness,
His legs kick out in futile spasm,

Head now whipping sadly sideways,
'Help me, help me, O Set help me!'

All the while his brother's laughter,
Rings and echoes through the temple,
Still the priest and pilgrim watch on,
They know a deeper tale unfolding.
Set hacks and cuts the joint in pieces,
Hurling body parts now hither,
To a thrilled crowd running forward,
For their trophy, their god's body,
Roar with frenzy, grabbing relics,
Catching parts of Sutekh's brother.

All the time Set works in gusto,
Chops his feet off to the ankles.

Then calves and knees and thigh joints,
Throws more out to greedy watchers,
Out they go now hitting nobles,
Staining fine white robes to crimson,
Blood falls like rubies through the temple.
Still the mad crowd surges forward,
Clamouring, shoving, screaming, shouting,
Set hears voices calling to him,
For the greatest prize of magick.
'I have given you the body
Of your dear and wondrous saviour.
Was not the thirteen pieces plenty?

Song of Merikhem

What other prizes do you crave for?'
Hears a voice call from the temple.
'Give us a charm, give us his member!'
The utmost charm of any great god
That will control the darkest forces
Control the caverns of the Apep.

'So you want the fourteenth segment?
The only fragment worth possessing,
The only piece left undiscovered,
Never found by sister Nephthys!'
Far abroad once Set had scattered
All the limbs of his lost brother,
Those that fell on Khemit's blackland,
Formed the power zones of worship.

But his phallus fell not earthward,
Went it to the watery Nile god,
To be eaten by a scaled fish,
Lodged forever in this being,
Thus this prize, Set denies them.

Still they raged and roared in frenzy,
'Give us the Talisman of Wasir!'
Set reached down through sodden linen
Of the blood-soaked limbless body,
Still he laughs in wild abandon
As the crowd begs 'Give it to us!
Give us the power of his phallus!'

From noble lords to beasts a' bellowing,
All their dignity disappearing,
Set ignores their pleas with pleasure,
Hacking off his brother's member.
'A gift!' he cries to Rameses second,
From one mighty god to another!
As God of Darkness, I give this phallus,
To the greatest in all Khemit!'

Hopping wildly down the stone steps,
Set now bounds toward his patron,
At the feet of Rameses second
Places Wasir's blood-soaked member.
Pharaoh gathers up this relic,
Breathing in and utters lowly,
'I feel the power surging through me!'

Spellbound 'neath the paint and powder,
Pharaoh smiles upon this phallus,
Believing it to be a symbol,
Holds it up for all to gaze on.

Set content, his gift accepted,
Returns to stage, to reap more havoc
On the dismembered other brother,
Still alive, but now in limbo,
From his eyes the tears are flowing,
Now his body shrunk and dwindled,
Drowning in a pool of life-blood,

Song of Merikhem

The final blow, his head was struck off.

Set holds up his closing trophy,
Wasir's tongue now hanging speechless,
But his eyes still swivel wildly,
Looks upon the world he once ruled,
As they dull, and now cloud over,
Set throws this head among his followers.

Ends the first act of this pageant.
Leaves an eager crowd in raptures,
Stained with blood, their clothes and faces,
Swelling clapping fills the temple,
Sending shocks through granite pillars,
Linen drapes now hide the killing.

Now the pilgrim joins the company,
Listens to the happy chatter,
Of the fine guests and the nobles,
All forgetting scenes of bloodshed,
Straightway they start their feasting,
Slaking thirst, and stilling hunger.
Rams' horns now beckon gentry,
As the audience take their places,
As the acting cast assembles,
A lone orator speaks forth clearly,
Of the murdering of Wasir,
Of the mourning of his sisters,
Of the lamenting of his passing,

Of the killing, by Set his brother.

When the linen curtains open,
Shows Set's sister Isis grieving,
Shows her finely veiled in linen,
Viewers awestruck by her beauty.

Gone now is the scene of horror,
As they gaze upon her presence,
As they look upon the goddess,
Shrouded now in deepest mystery,
This goddess now begins lamenting,
Long lamenting, loudly calling,
Through the dimness of the temple,
Torchlight catches on her headdress,
Darts and flickers on the metal.

Pharaoh's spellbound by her beauty,
Eyes transfixed upon her veiled face,
Still she sings about her sad loss.

'My heart is like a wounded song-bird,
In the thicket of a thorn bush,
There is no sweetness in the honey,
No more fragrance in the lotus,
My soul is thus an empty temple,
Deserted by my god and lover.'
Pharaoh's wives now fall to weeping,
But no one pays attention to them.

SONG OF MERIKHEM

'I look upon death's face sadly,
I pray a second god may follow,
If he could lead me to my lover,
Let his loving warmth surround me,
Like the vapour of the morning.'

Her words of beauty all too perfect,
For this mighty crowd assembled,
Fall to weeping, broken-hearted,
Are the men in Pharaoh's party
Tears now cutting through their makeup.

Pharaoh blinks his darkened eyelids,
Cause for bitter tears and murmurs,
Comes on stage the goddess Nephthys,
Sings a duet with her sister,
Hand in hand they search for fragments,
Of the body of their brother,
Of the mutilated actor
That played Osiris with such passion.

His body parts were quickly gathered,
By the priests at intermission,
But the most prized of all, his member,
Pharaoh grasps still in his right hand.

Thus the priestly make exception,
And allow his shade to pass on,
Through the many gated hallways

To the netherworld of Apep.

As the sisters search and gather,
All the thirteen chopped up pieces,
Sing their songs so heavy hearted,
In praise of Wasir's sacred body.

'May your hands and feet be bless'ed,
May your limbs and trunk be bless'ed,
May your noble head be bless'ed,
May your dead eyes shine like torches,
Glitter like the stars in heaven,
Eyes that shine in gentle beauty,
And shine forever with our father,
Death shall never dim such beauty,
Nor your mummy wrappings bind you.'

When at last the sisters finish,
Finish many linen wrappings,
Once again begin their wailing,
'We have lost our precious treasure!'
Thus poor Isis wails in sorrow,
'Woe is me, my life is empty,
Without his phallus life is fruitless,
Help me solve this frustration,
One of us must make the magick.'
Audience stirs now leaning forward,
Thus intrigued by Isis' notion,
She continues, but now scheming:

Song of Merikhem

'Let us steal from Sutekh's treasure,
Let us take the gold from Nubty,
We can make a golden member,
From the magick molten metal.'
Then the curtain lowers gently.

Now with great appeal to listeners,
Of incest! And necrophilia!
Of gods and men, there's no distinction.
So the viewers sit there waiting,
Lusting after more sensation.

The linen curtain rises slowly,
To an eager audience waiting,
Nervous laughter quickly muffled,
Then the stage is dimly backlit,
Behind a filmy gauzy curtain,
Stands a semi-naked figure,
Is this Isis in her mystery?

Touched by beauty from the heavens,
Slowly peeling off her garment,
In a sensuous wanton manner,
Cheers erupting in the temple,
Urging her to show her body,
Looks upon the form in shadow,
Now gyrating in the torchlight.
Appears Osiris bound in linen,
A golden member now protruding,

The viewers gasp in admiration.

'Look, his manhood is restoreth!'

Isis stroking now the member,
Causing it to grow much longer.
The audience loves it, loves it better,
When Isis mounts her brother-lover.
'So real is this performer's acting!
And her virtual seventh heaven!'
The crowd cries out in adoration,
'She's not an actress! She's a fornicator!'

At the climax of this union,
Darkness fills Great Sety's temple,
Merging from the dim of shadow,
Isis walks towards the centre.
'I have born a son immortal,
To the great and good Osiris,
Who rests in darkness under Khemit.'

In her arms an infant new born,
Presents it to the god Osiris,
'Greet the young and tender baby,
God of wind, sky and heavens.'

Linen curtains once more lowered,
Horus Followers roar in tumult,
As the second act concluded

Song of Merikhem

More recitations are delivered.

As the final act commenceth,
Slowly raised the filmy linen
To a scene beside the river,
Isis sits there with handmaidens,
Her wet robe clings to her body,
Glistens in the flickering torchlight.

Horus enters from the wing side,
In his polished warrior's armour,
Stands before his mother Isis,
God and goddess show their beauty,
Bathe in the viewer's adoration.

He relates his tales of battle,
To his fascinated mother,
To the fascinated listeners,
More applause thus erupting,
And more cheering swirls about him,
Pharaoh throws out lotus blossoms
To the proud and handsome actor.

Isis interrupts now singing,
Of the sufferings of Wasir:
'What now the fate upon our household?
The curse of Set is here upon us,
Go seek out your monstrous uncle,
You will know him by his cunning,

'By his arrogance and bloodlust,
By his fiery flock of red-locks,
By his fierce and flashing gold sword.

'Use the magick I have taught you,
Of the binding and the sorcery,
With the silken threads of power,
Bind him chain him to our willing,
Fetter him in chains of magick.
So that all the gods may wander,
Wander they in perfect freedom,
Knowing neither strife nor problem.'

Isis leaves the stage still singing,
Sings a well-loved piece of music,
Looks ahead, and eager watching,
Humming in anticipation.

With a crash, Set comes a'leaping,
For the cataclysmic battle.
He is greeted with such hatred,
By the fickle hearted viewers.

Still he swaggers forward proudly,
In his hands he cups his member,
Thrusting out his hips in mock'ry,
Making many obscene gestures,
To the frustration of the viewers,
Driving all men wild with fury,

Song of Merikhem

'Kill him! Kill him!' howl the men folk.
'Smash his face, rip out his gizzards!'
Anger grows, more cries for vengeance.

Across the flagstones Set now swaggers
Sauntering, making obscene gestures,
Says to the actor playing Horus:
'Who is this child who stands before me?'
Surveying him with speculation.
'I am Horus, son of Wasir!'

Set now mocks with peals of laughter,
'Pray what is it you are seeking?
Boy child of this dead Osiris.'
'I seek vengeance for my father
I seek the murderer of Osiris.'
'Search no further!' Sutekh screams out,
'For I am he who rid the black land,
Of the stasis and the rotting,
Of the putrid and decaying,
In the likeness of Osiris!'

Sharpen well their trusty weapons,
Rush together, clashing metal,
Chest to chest blades locked together.
'Should you still desire to fight me?'
Hisses the all-powerful Sutekh,
'I am skilled in arts of warfare!'
He answers to his angry uncle,

'When your wisdom calls for fighting,
Clever thinking, cunning Sutekh,
You just bring more pain and sorrow,
I am champion for all virtues!'

Now the viewers' mood turns fiery,
As the two fight on in combat,
Thrusting, cutting, fiercely parrying,
Blades now whirling, glinting brightly,
Quick the hero-swords are tested,
And the blades are rightly measured,
Sending sounds throughout the temple,
Like the heavy ring of hammers,
Created by the metal maker,
Forged for them to make their magick.

Quickly pushing Horus backwards,
Lunging now towards his helmet,
Slashes Horus in his right eye,
Sending hot blood spurting outwards,
Now his right eye rendered useless,
Blindly stabbing through the night air,
Set attacks him even further,
Prods and gouges at his right thigh,
Nicks his biceps, then his right arm.
Horus weaving, parrying ducking,
Set now grunting in pure pleasure,
As his nephew fights for victory.
But Set keeps up his speed and fury,

Horus & Set: The Great Battle

Shows no pity to his nephew.

A roar goes throughout the temple,
As the battle grows more vicious.

Set lunges for the throat of Horus,
But he now steps quickly sideways,
To divert this fateful sword stroke,
Two blades meet, metal clashing.
Set's blade snaps off to the pommel,
Horus's blade is still undamaged,
Set's strong arm now crashing downwards,
Sends his nephew's sword out flying.

Now the two are locked together,
Crushing embrace of arms uniting,
Whirling, spinning round in circles,
Leaping over bloodied flagstones,
Aiming to push Set off-balance,
Wildly glaring at each other,
On their faces mars defiance,
Within Set's heart the grudge of ages,
His ancestral thirst for vengeance,
His hereditary hatred.
Now the air is full of shouting,
Gone the mock of playful actors,
Now the pilgrim senses fury,
'This is no normal battle,
Of a nephew towards an uncle,

But a battle for true godhead!'

With the shattered sword of gold ore,
Set strikes out at Heru's forehead,
Reddened with much blood outpouring,
Heru twists avoiding Sutekh,
Like a python Heru strikes out,
Life and death he then encircles,
Till Sutekh is crushed to pieces,
Till the air is dark with misery,
Now Sutekh's lungs explode,
Gives a scream of pain and suff'ring.

For a moment Set now wavers,
Fixes his golden eyes on Heru,
But Heru draws his dagger swiftly,
Plunges it through Sutekh's body,
Hilt hard up against his backbone,
Making Set now turn more livid.
Pharaoh whispers to his Sem Priest,
'This would have killed a lesser mortal!'
Set gives a shout, a cry of anguish,
Then skids across the stony paving.

With a heave of upper body,
Sutekh falls down crashing backwards,
Twisting on the broken blade head,
Cracking ribs and splintering breastbone,
Hitting head and cracking cranium,

Till at last he falls defeated,
His last breath now whistles outwards,
Gives a final scream in anger,
Has no more strength to lift his body.

The crowd is seized now by this mocking,
'Kill him!' roar the maddened viewers.

Retrieving his discarded weapon,
Lifting bloodied sword up highly,
Horus rages round his uncle,
Smears of blood upon his forehead,
Down his sides and back and shoulders.

Soaking chest hair and staining clothing,
Painted is he with this blood-paint,
Face contorted like a death mask,
Holds the sword right over Sutekh,
Plunging bloodied sword down fiercely,
Impales forever Sutekh's carcass.

'Thus I bind you with this magick,
May you wander thus forever!
Wander eastward wander westward,
May you drift upon the north wind
Find no peace down in the southland,
Isolation is your password,
You are condemned to lasting chaos,
Live out your life in blind confusion,

Song of Merikhem

'I expel you from the sunlight,
Spend forever in dark places.

'I give you rule o'er thief and coward,
Over liars, and the murderers,
Over robbers and violators,
To all the evil and blasphemers.

'Breakers of the faith in Wasir,
From henceforth you're god of evil,
Carry with you Curse of Horus,
Sut-Typhon's your name forever!

'I have resurrected my dear father,
Given back the great peacemaker,
Given back the lord of white-light,
Now restored and lives forever,
Ever lasting peace in stasis,
May Osiris live forever!
What more could his people ask for?'

So the pilgrim sits in silence,
Ponders many inward questions,
Kha'em looks at her expectant.

'This is too much! I'll not be silent!'
Cries out Meri-Khem in outrage.
'What a farce, what dishonour!
How could Sutekh let this happen?'

With much reserve he now answered,
'But this is what the people wanted,
A mere scapegoat, for a puppet,
Released is Wasir for the masses.'

Not content with Kha'em's answer,
'Is your family not of Sutekh?
Did they not follow Shaitan proudly?
Were renowned among the fighters,
And for triumphs in the battle,
For the profit of the people,
For advantage of the nation?
And Sety built a shrine for praying,
Built a temple in the desert,
By the shining Hapuy River!'

Now returning to the pageant -
Thus does Pharaoh leave the temple,
Glancing at the bloody pave stones,
Still holds on to Sutekh's member,
Thinking on this awful folly,
Of the raging of this Heru,
Of the raging of his people,
Now what will the future offer?
If we release this dreaded stasis?
Nay, it will not last forever,
Folk are wise, not so stupid,
They'll not follow in his footsteps,
They'll seek chaos and confusion,

SONG OF MERIKHEM

Not a road of soothing calmness.

So contented with his reasoning,
Bids the company health and prosper,
Bids goodnight to all his nobles,
And the priesthood of the temple,
Walks out into Abju's night sky,
Towards another Khemit day.

Chapter Twelve
Journey to Fayum

So they journey northward, northward,
Left behind the fields of killing,
Left behind the Wasir followers,
Crossed the rushing Hapuy River,
Crossed the desert dry and dusty,
Passed the many mud brick dwellings,
Passed the many solar temples.

So the pilgrim travelled onwards,
In the guidance of her Sem Priest,
Kha'emwaset, son of Rameses,
Follower of the great god Sutekh.

All the while the pilgrim travelled,
Felt a strangeness, in her gullet,
Felt the blue in her throat centre,
Felt the rising of this blue ray,
For a moment saw the starlight,
Saw the star of Megrez rising.

Far above her head now spinning,
In the dark sky of the goddess,
Filled her every moving moment,
Caps her head in multi auras,
'This is but a taste of heaven,'

SONG OF MERIKHEM

Kha'em whispers to her softly,
'Let us journey further northward,
To the land of ancient Sobek,
To the ancient town of Ta-she,
To the mystery of the mazes,
Where many souls are lost in wandering.'

Meri-Khem now halted, sat down,
'Tell me more about these mazes,
Why do souls get lost in wandering?
Who created all these mazes?'
Kha'em answered, he did tell her:
'Great were the many Amon-em-hets,
Ancient kings who worshipped Sobek,
Who built a many room'ed structure,
Three thousand rooms all dark and sombre.

'Each one with its Neter's symbol,
With its own ancestral emblem,
Many tunnels, many hallways,
Going leftward, going rightward.'
'Tell me more please?' asked the pilgrim.

'Twelve roofed courts, with doors a'facing,
Six to northward, six to southward,
In a straight line they continue,
Double sets and double chambers,
Some are earthward some are hidden,
Half above and half below.

'Now rest Meri do not ponder,
May your dreams be visions many.'

Chapter Thirteen
The Labyrinth

After resting, gathering spirit,
Many days they walked together,
Till they came to Lake Sher-re-sy,
Groves of date palms lined the water
That added contrast to the desert.

As Meri looked across the vast lake,
Stood and gazed upon the waters,
'What is this I see before me?
What is moving in these waters?'

'In this sacred Lake Sher-re-sy,
Are the very special reptiles,
They are fed and be-jewell-ed,
By the many Sobek wa-habs.
From the crocodiles is taken,
Special oil for royal anointing,
Sacred is this oil of mesech,
That anoints the kings of Egypt,
That will be sacred to all king-ship,
And make its mark for future regents.

'Beside the lake was built a structure,
See the pyramid before you,
Many are the reddened mud bricks,

Rising upwards, rising skyward,
To the gleaming blue above us.'

As they walked towards the structure,
Guardians come forth from its shadows.
Stood before them, barred the entrance
'Halt! You must come no further!
Forbidden are these ancient dwellings,
In them buried, are the Pharaohs,
May they dwell here and wander,
Through the many rooms a'winding.
They built this labyrinth to Sobek,
To this noble god of mystery,
Cousin to the dark god Sutekh.'
Kha'em gestured to these keepers

SONG OF MERIKHEM

Sobek

Speaking in a lowly whisper,
'I am Keeper of the Secrets,
I am Master of the Mysteries,
I am Prince Setne Kha'emwaset,
And I bring a pilgrim with me,
One who seeks initiation.'

They look at him with eyes of wonder.
But they questioned not the Sem Priest,
Then they muttered to each other,
Thus agreed to let her enter.

'Let us welcome then the pilgrim.'
'I pray thee, you may enter inwards,
Walk among the ancient Neters,
Marvel at the pillared hallways,
Pause in courtyards many splendid.'

They stood aside and bade her enter,
Here stands the maze in all its splendour.

Through the great door of the complex,
Walked the pilgrim gravely thinking,
'They've left me here alone to wander
No one to guide me through this chaos,
No one to help me solve this puzzle,'

Downward through the murky blackness,
Reeling downwards to the bottom,

SONG OF MERIKHEM

Hitting head and bruising shoulders,
Falling into deepest chasms,
'Is there no one who can help me?'

But no helper hears her calling.
Many corridors do beckon,
Crypts and caverns winding tunnels,
Then a crashing all around her
Like a splitting in the heavens.
Cried he in a voice of thunder,
Cried the spirit of the tunnels,
In a tone so loudly scorning,
'Hasten back now to your city,
Back to all who are faint hearted,
You have no business in these mazes!'

'You do not scare me!' cries the pilgrim,
'I will continue with my venture,
I will find the inner sanctum,
I will be my guide in darkness.'

Nothing daunted, fearing nothing,
So our pilgrim moves in blackness,
She is touched by spirits many,
Feels their soft hands, hears their whispers
Speak a language of the old ones,
Takes her backwards to her first time.

Then a spirit swooped upon her,

With his finger on her temple whispered,
'This is not the right time Meri,
Listen to your inner heartbeat.
Find the element of healing,
Gather all the words of wisdom,
From the great ones in the darkness.

'For it is said of this dark place,
That all the Nomes assembled yearly,
Ranked together priest and priestess,
Offering gifts up to the Neters,
Giving justice of great import.'

Voices echoed through the hallways,
Telling her of ancient past times,
She now feels the fleeting phantoms,
Feels them slithering round her body
Like the serpent, the Great Apophis,
Very crafty, very cunning,
'Is this the creeping stealth of Evil?'

From the empty air appearing,
Found an arch above a doorway,
Drawn and painted on this entrance
Were many coded secret letters.

'Life is white, and death is darkened,
Life and death are drawn in circles,
Ever-decreasing winding circles.

Song of Merikhem

'What are the meanings of these symbols?
I must solve this ancient puzzle,
Anti-clockwise I must venture,
To unwind my tired body.'

She feels a sagging like a sky-cloud,
Bends and makes a noise beneath her
On this dizzy swimming earth-scape.
Confusing mass of dismal alleys,
She meanders, she just wanders,
Loses senses of direction,
Down a narrow passage onwards,
Stumbles headlong through the shadows,
Sees no more the wandering spirits,
Hears no more their inner ravings,
Just listens to the drum of silence.

Through un-interrupted silence,
She hears the magick, hears the secrets,
Very sleepy with the silence,
Lies down on her bed of silence,
In the centre of the labyrinth,
In the centre of an island
Burns the dark light, burns the black flame,
Of the everlasting torchlight,
Whispers to her in her slumbers,
 'In the land of concrete-jungle,
Still the voice of Set would reach you!'
Standing proudly, adorned and regal,

Holds the Uwas in Sutekh's likeness,
Appears Lord Sobek from the shadows.
'I am the oldest of the Neters,
Ask of me all you search for,
But speak in riddles speak in my tongue,
Lest all others hear the secrets,
Lest they betray your very reasoning.'
So the pilgrim uttered soul sounds,
Spake the ancient tongue of Sobek,
Then the figures flashed before her,
Each one in a separate chamber,
All was written in these figures,
In each one a special meaning,
Each its separate charm recorded.

Many thousand names were written.
Sobek speaks in tongue to Meri,
'Learn their names and all their secrets,
Charms of medicine charms of magick,
Hear the magick in your naming,
All its mystery in its singing.'

Thus her name becomes her password,
Bridges earth, sky and heaven,
From the land of Sleep and Silence,
Awakes the pilgrim from the dream state.
Sobek reigns, Sobek has beckoned,
Retracing clockwise prior footsteps,
Traces winding pathways forward,

Song of Merikhem

Pathways through the darkened chambers.

Hears the whispers from these shadows,
Hears the crying from the darkness,
Lost are these souls to wander,
Those who did not make the journey,
Each one pleading 'Take me with you,
Meri! Meri take me with you.'

These are but her thoughts discarded,
Worn out memories of her old life,
Of her death and now renewal,
Onwards, onwards she now travels,
Out of chaos and confusion,
Into harmony and order,
Of her mind, and now her notions.

Kha'emwaset is there to greet her,
He regards her proudly saying,
'I salute you now My Priestess.'

Standing taller in the sunshine,
Near the shadow of the mazes,
Of the great testing inner sanctum,
From the heartland of the Spirit
Meri stood there finer, wiser.
'Your mind is likened to this warren,
Like a many room'ed palace,
Many pilgrims know their limits,

Visit only just a few rooms,
Leave the rest all cloaked in darkness,
Never open up the windows.

'Unlike those who went before you
You have been to all these spaces,
In your mind and in the mazes,
You stood erect and made your pledges.

'Now with your mind of magick,
You will travel ever onwards,
Into heaven's upper spaces,
Into Nu'it's starry pastures,
You have found the source of healing.'

Chapter Fourteen
Kha'emwaset

Seven days and nights they rested,
Raised their eyes to Ursa Major,
Phecda shining down upon them,
Looked with thanks up to the stellar,
Looked on high in joy and gladness.

On the morning of the eighth day
While the pilgrim still lay sleeping,
And the fog lay on the river,
Kha'emwaset held up his sceptre,
Casts his spell across the river,
Spake the tongue of ancient Khemit.

'Ye inen makhent en Henu,
Rud akit em mehit,
Em Khentik er she neserser,
Em netcher khert.'

O'er the drowsy head of Meri,
To her ear there came a murmur
Just like waves upon a sea shore,
Just like winds among the palm trees,
He brings the boat of Henu earthward.

On the prow is standing Sutekh,

Standing proudly in the sunrise.
'We are away! Awake my priestess!
We travel now upon the light waves,
On the Henu boat for Neters,
We now sail for Lower Khemit.

'As we journey to Men-nefer,
Between Upper and Lower Khemit,
We link conscious, with unconscious,
As you awake your gland pineal,
Element of inspiration,
Your sixth sense will then awaken.

'As we sail there, I will tell you,
Of my life and all its meaning,
It is not a tale of wonder,
Or of some bizarre adventure,
But a tale of me, the king's son,
Fourth of Rameses the second,
Wed to Isit-Nefert my Great Mother.

'As a youth I fought in Nub-i-a,
I was not suited for this combat,
More versed was I in old magick,
Groomed for study not for killing.
Then I joined the Ptah temple,
Second only to the High Priest,
I was more than just a shaman,
I am Sem to my royal father,

Song of Merikhem

'Hem-Neter I was thus named
"He who justly serves all Neters."

'I am Khemit's man of mystery,
I can travel out of body,
I can bring back information,
In a trance state I do journey.
I am seer when Khemit battles,
And many battles Rameses headed.

'Now today I am the High Priest
In my life I guard the Pharaoh,
As his son, and his High Priest,
Guardian of The Sacred Bundle,
This I always carry for him
During all his Heb Sed trials,
All throughout his sacred office.'

Meri-Khem just sat and listened,
But she had a question for him,
'What is this special sacred bundle
That you carry for your father?'

'At the birth of my royal father,
Taken from him his royal placenta,
Dwelling in this foetal organ,
Is the child's eternal spirit.
Dried and wrapped in whitest linen,
It is placed within a coffer,

'Fixed high upon a regal standard,
And carried in the great procession,
Of the Heb Sed of renewal.

'This is a very ancient custom,
Carried by a Priest of Sutekh,
Guardian of the Royal Placenta,
Keeper of the Sacred Bundle,
On the evening of his Heb Sed.

'In great pomp and ceremony,
I will open this Royal Bundle,
And recite the ancient blessings,
For renewal of my sovereign,
May he live long, and for ever.'

'O Set, great in deity,
Make the sovereign King more glorious,
May you look upon Kha'emwaset,
Pharaoh's Son, and his protector,
Cause me to be much stronger,
May he live through Great Lord Sutekh,
I am my father's keeper,
I, who know the road of passing,
And the resting place beyond here.
I am he who raiseth Hadit,
I am he who guards the Nek-heh,
I can strengthen him above all,
I will sleep upon the Great Thigh,

Song of Merikhem

I shall open up Sokaris,
In the womb of Nut is magick,
I open up the Royal Placenta,
And causeth him to take his first breath.
All your enemies' arms are seiz'ed,
Glorious as the lord of Ta-Wer,
Life, well being in thy temple,
For I am thy son, and your protector.'

Meri-Khem sat and gazed at Kha'em,
Looked with pride upon his beauty,
At his tall and graceful figure,
'He carries charms of all magicians
From the past into the future,
All the magick powers of Sutekh.'

She felt blessed, she felt enchanted,
Received her sign of inspiration,
Words held magick virtues in them,
Meri murmured, she did whisper:
'O my Kha'em, my true beloved.'
Kha'em thus continued speaking:
'I am my father's royal protector,
And I am his executioner,
If his strength and vigour fail him,
I will perform a ritual slaughter.'
Meri looked in horror at him.
'Kha'em I find this practice awful!'

'It was accepted by the people,
That the shaman or the Sem Priest,
Should be called upon by council,
To kill the king or tribal leader,
If he failed to do his duty,
Mortally wounded in high battle,
Or grew old, and passed his prime life.

'But our family never did this,
Many kings who followed Wasir,
They would always choose a scapegoat,
Would seek out the fair skinned people,
Seek out uncommon redheads,
Those who resembled Sutekh,
They would be the sacrificial,
They would be the blood of Pharaoh,
Chosen for their evil colouring.

'Red was but an evil omen,
To have the red hair of our great god,
My Grandfather, the Great Sety,
Had Set's flames upon his proud head,
Had the hair that others frowned on.

'But my Grandfather did not honour
These old ways of Lord Osiris.
He embraced the ways of Sutekh,
He did not support this killing.'

SONG OF MERIKHEM

Meri touched her red hair thinking:
'I would not be spared in ancient Khemit!'

Chapter Fifteen
Journey to Men-nefer

As they glided in the Henu,
On the pure waves of sunlight,
From the waters and the marshes,
Rose the wild duck and the heron.

'We shall venture to Men-nefer,
There to greet Ptah-Sokar,
Father of Men-nefer Triad.'

'Who is this Men-nefer Triad?'
Asked the priestess to Kha'emwaset.

'Ne-fer-tum, Ptah and Sekhmet,
Nefer came forth from the lotus,
Cherished boy child of Great Sekhmet.
To the sun it gives protection,
But when the night-sky overtakes it,
The lotus sends forth heady fragrance.

'Like a many-petaled lotus,
Is your central nervous system.
May your wisdom ever-flower
As you come into your being.

'Let us leave our boat of pure light,

SONG OF MERIKHEM

Ptah image by Billie Walker-John

And journey forth to old Men-nefer,
Surrounds this city is Ineb-Hedj,
An ancient white wall of pure limestone,
Built by Aha, known as Men-es,
In the great age of expansion,
So was built a royal city,
And to Ptah a solar temple,
Great and justly is this wise god.

'My father Rameses has a statue,
A monumental feat in granite,
That towers up, grandly skywards.

'All around is green and grassy,
Grows the maize-fields, lush and shining,
Grows the barley golden yellow,
Filling all the land with plenty.

'Tis the fellahin who in Proyet,
Plant the broad fields and the orchards,
To be harvested in Shemu,
To make the amber beer and corn bread,
And in the temple built for Rameses,
We make libations to the deity.

'Come let us now walk to the temple
You can then see Ptah-Sokar.'

In a shrine, within this temple,

'Stood the statue of the wise one.
On his head a turquoise blue cap,
Glowing deeply in the faint light.
He is robed in golden raiment,
Scaled and filmy like a serpent,
In his hands he grasps his wand stick,
Multi-formed and multi-layered,
Wrought in blackest of the metals,
Glinting here and there a gold trim.
Ankh, Djed and Uwas sceptre,
Life, Stability, and Endurance.

'When Amenti calls my father,
He aids us in our ceremony,
An ancient ritual of mouth opening
Breathing life to give him power,
Cheating death, restoring beauty
So the king may live forever.'
Meri looks upon this idol:
'He is not tall or grand in stature,
But he is a curious image,
Surveys me with his eyes of emerald.'

'Ah!' she cries 'He looks right through me!
I can feel his piercing green eyes
Meeting mine within his darkness.
From whence was Ptah-Sokar fashioned?'

Kha'em lays his hand upon her

Speaks these words to priestess Meri,
'He was not created, but simply is.'

Chapter Sixteen
The Serapeum

Along an avenue of Sphinxes,
From the great Ptah Temple,
Walks the priestess and the Sem Priest,
Passing many ancient structures,
All restored and documented,
By this Sem Priest, Kha'emwaset,
He who also wrote the history,
Of the ancient Kings of Khemit.

He thus tells her of his working,
Of this lore and understanding.

'You'll be great one day in Khemit.'
Says the priestess to Kha'emwaset
But he shakes his head in sadness
'I will be cheated of my birthright,
By a king who will outlive me.'

Kha'emwaset thus continued:
'As Royal Keeper of the Secrets,
And as Master of the Threshold,
I have built a place of resting,
Usir-Hapuy, my father named it,
For the black bull, called the Apis.
Come now Meri, I will show you.'

Down a stony granite stairway,
Go the priestess and the Sem Priest
To the entrance of a dark crypt.
Kha'em reaches into the shadows
Making flames to light the darkness.

Along a passageway they enter,
Turning left and going downwards,
Niches carved into the limestone
Hold the many votive off'rings.

Turning left they pass a coffin,
To an ancient king now passed on,
Then comes the foremost gallery,
Likened to a great cathedral,
Flanking left and flanking rightward
Are the many Apis chambers,
Hewn out of solid bedrock,
For the sacred bulls there buried.

'Twenty eight are they in number,
Each one has a separate coffer,
All engraved and highly polished,
Each named for this sacred Apis,
They were worshipped they are sacred,
Harking back to times primeval
To an earlier Age of Taurus,
Starry cluster in the night-sky,
Just above the field of Sahu

SONG OF MERIKHEM

Khaem with Apis bull

So the bull was manifested.'

Kha'emwaset thus continues:
'In the many ritual gath'rings,
We still parade and decorate him,
With the lilies of the lake lands,
And the poppies of the pasture,
In the middle of his forehead
A golden disc is thus surmounted,
Then led by Pharaoh and the Sem Priest
Through Men-nefer to the temple.

'Like a god the bull is buried
Embalmed and wrapped in finest linen,
Incense burns in copper vestals,
Prayers are uttered by the priestly,
Gathered are the many mourners,
Shedding tears and cries of sorrow.'
Meri touched with much emotion
Feeling tears upon her pale cheeks.
Kha'em leads the priestess outwards,
Outwards to the brilliant sunshine,
Past the ancient sandstone structures,
To the pyramid of Zoser.

Chapter Seventeen
Journey to Saqqara

In the forecourt of this temple
Many noble lords and ladies,
With their servants in attendance,
Crowds of people mass together,
Gathering are they by the hundreds,
Scribes and priesthoods from the temples,
Paying homage to their deities,
Burning incense for their favour.

Much excitement fills this quarter
As banners fly in multi-colours.
'What is happ'ning?' asks the priestess,
'Why the people, why the banners?'
'During the sacred month of Khoiak,
When the Hapuy River shrivels,
Is the signal of the Heb Sed
A celebration of renewal,
Of the king for all his subjects.

'I must leave you my dear Meri,
To prepare my king for ritual,
For his trial of strength and vigour.'
All is hushed as trumpets fanfare,
Retinues of priests surge forward,
Many coloured are their raiment,

Priests of Sutekh, Priests of Horus,
On the courtyard of Saqqara
Each prepares a separate temple,
Flying high the double banners
Red, white and golden yellow.

Then an avenue is opened,
Lined with Karnak's chosen priesthood,
To a constant thudding drumbeat,
Gazing only at the gold throne,
Pharaoh walking stately forwards.

Many hours he walks in pageant,
With the statues and the Sem Priest,
Kha'em walks before his sovereign,
Carrying forth the Royal Placenta,
Carrying forth his Sacred Bundle.

Wears the leopard skin of office.
Firmly grasping in his right hand,
Kha'em holds the gold Ur-Hekau.
As he treads the soft sands slowly,
Leading Rameses to the dais,
Royal attendees and fan-bearers,
Move aside for Pharaoh's Sem Priest,
Make solemn pledges to their sovereign,
Who now sits upon a gold throne.

His feet are washed in ancient practice,

Song of Merikhem

A Sem Priest

Empowered prayers and chants are uttered,
Khyphi incense waft around him,
Oil of Sobek smeared upon him,
Thus anointed, leaves the dais
With his Sem Priest, Kha'emwaset,
Continues to the room for robing.
Kha'em makes a further blessing,
Upon his Father, Mighty Rameses.

In the centre of the courtyard,
Stands the double throne of Khemit,
Double is this ancient kingdom,
Double is the Heb Sed ritual,
Twinning is the king's pavilion,
On the courtyard of Saqqara.
Now the king processes forward,
Alternate sittings on the two thrones,
Wearing Hedjet then the Deshert,
Crowns of Upper and Lower Khemit,
Wearing white, and then the red robe,
Asserting power o'er the black land,
And his hopes to reign forever.

He walks across temple courtyard,
Carried then upon a litter,
Preceded by the falcon standard,
To the sacred Horus Chapel.

From his Sem Priest, Kha'emwaset,

SONG OF MERIKHEM

Receives the flail, crook and sceptre
Wrapped in a white linen
And four times stated:

'Mighty Bull, with plumes so lofty,
Favourite of the Two Goddesses,
Great in Kingship in Temple Karnak,
Golden Hawk god, Circlet wearer,
From the regions of the south-wind,
King of Upper and Lower Khemit.
Beauty is the being of Heru,
The Only One of Mighty Heru
Son of the Sun, Order of Amon,
Divine Ruler of earth and heaven,
Great in Duration, Beloved of Horus
Living for Ever, Ever and Ever.'

Receiving homage from his subjects,
With many blessings from the old ones,
Making generous off'rings to them,
Then removes his cloak of white wool,
Leaves the chapel, built to Heru,
Clad in just a kilt of linen
With his false tail sweeps the sand-floor,
Dons the crown of Upper Khemit.
Carries a whisk and golden sceptre,
Four times runs around the courtyard,
Returns now to the Heru Chapel,
Offers up his royal insignia,

Makes more off'rings to this deity,
Is carried then upon a litter
To the sacred Sutekh Chapel.

From his Sem Priest, Kha'emwaset
Receives flail, crook and sceptre,
Cloaked in red and four times stated:

'Mighty Bull, with plumes so lofty,
Favourite of the Two Goddesses,
Great in Kingship in Temple Karnak ,
Golden Jackal, Circlet wearer,
From the regions of the north-wind,
King of Upper and Lower Khemit.
Beauty is the being of Sutekh,
The Only One of Mighty Sutekh,
Son of the Stars, Pride of Nu'it,
Divine Ruler of earth and heaven,
Great in Duration, Beloved of Sutekh
Living for Ever, Ever and Ever.'

Receiving homage from his subjects,
With many blessings from the old ones,
Making generous off'rings to them,
Then removes his cloak of red wool,
Dons the crown of Lower Khemit,
Carries whisk, and golden sceptre,
Leaves the chapel, built to Sutekh,
With his false tail sweeps the sand-floor.

Song of Merikhem

Repeats the marathon o'er again,
All the day he runs the gamut,
All the day he changes his garments,
Forth into the flush of sunset,
Paying homage to these two gods,
Heru-Sutekh, twinning brothers,
Concludes the testing feats of vigour.

He re-visits sacred temples,
Horus of Behdet, Set of Ombos,
He has proved his strength and kingship,
Makes more off'rings to the two gods,
Washes, oils and changes garments,
Dons the Khepresh, greatest war crown,
Dons his breastplate, and his gauntlet,
Takes his quiver and bow of Cypress,
Returning to the field of proving.

Raises this mighty bow of Cypress,
Seizes arrows, metal headed,
Golden trumpets sound a fanfare,
There he shoots these victory arrows,
To four corners of his kingdom.
To the pomp of sacred music
Kha'emwaset steps now forward
To the tumult of the people,
Spake these words to Pharaoh Rameses:
'Ankh ankh, en mit-ak,
Yewk er heh en heh,

Aha en heh.'

'Live life, thou shalt not die,
Thou shalt exist for a million years
For millions of millions of years.'

Thus does finish Pharaoh's trial,
Re-enacting his enthroning,
Proud Heru thus judged him justly,
Great Sutekh thus judged him wisely
Ancient is this celebration,
Pharaoh's Heb Sed of renewal.

Chapter Eighteen
Opening of Mouth Ceremony

Far from moonlight and the starlight,
Deep within the great masta-ba,
In the structure built by Zoser,
Is a chamber deeply hidden,
Carefully chosen is this chamber
For Opening of the Mouth Ce-remony.

A retinue of priests assemble,
Meri-Khem thus follows closely,
To witness an unusual practice,
That of Rameses, King of Khemit.

In this chamber, by a torchlight,
Standing on a mound of gold ore,
Prepared is Rameses for his rebirth,
Prepared and bearded is this Pharaoh,
Wrapped in finest whitest linen
Like a mummy, like Udi-mu.

All the priests are gathered round him,
Burn the incense in the chamber,
Wahabs utter sacred vowel sounds,
Countless are the many echoes,
Flap like buzzards in their eyries.

Chilling cold breath fills the dank air,
Come the death cries of the slaughtered,
Of a bull, duck and deerling,
From the bull, the heart is taken,
Cuts the foreleg from its quarters,
Cuts the head of duck and deerling,
Is then carried by the butcher.

Says the Kher-Heb to the Sem Priest:
'For Temu thus, I have seized them.'

Presents thigh and heart to Pharaoh:
'Brought unto thee the mark of Sutekh,
Brought unto the Eye of Horus,
Brought unto thee heads of forfeit.'
Thus the sacrifices ended.

All the while the priestess watches,
Breathes the sacred air of Pharaoh.
'I should feel strange about this ritual
I only know I am no stranger
I re-member this old practice.'

In the shadows of this chamber,
Lurks a covered form of mystery,
Sacred Ka sign wrapped in Meska,
Hides the figure of Tek-en-u,
Standing on a sled of timber,
He awaits his call from Pharaoh,

SONG OF MERIKHEM

As his soul retains its rebirth,
Like a doorway he will open,
So that Pharaoh can pass through it.

Like the sun through Nu-it's body,
Every evening as the sun sets
So the Ka performs its duty,
Ever quiet ever present,
Ever watchful over Pharaoh.

Next the adze is thus presented
To the Pharaoh this is offered.
Speaks the Sem Priest to his father:
'Now your eyes and mouth are opened,

'By thy Adze, and mark of Sutekh,
I, your son Heru-Sutekh,
I have pressed your mouth to open,
May you utter words of Sutekh.'
Says the Kher-Heb, stepping forward:
'I present you with the Seb-Hur,
Mighty instrument of Anpu,
May your eyes be ever open.
Thus your mouth and eyes are opened.'

With the Adze and mighty Seb-Hur,
Censes once more Pharaoh's body,
With the quema from far Nekhen.
Says the Kher-Heb, stepping forward:

'Thou art pure, thou art Sutekh,
May thou receive the gold Ur-Hekau,
Of the great ophidian current.'

Behind the king now stands the Sem Priest,
Offers him the royal Meshenti,
Regal crown of Great Lord Sutekh.

'I illumine thus your forehead,
I incense your head with natron,
Now I offer you four boxes,
All part of your ritual cleansing,
Now you have your eyes wide open,
Now you have your mouth wide open.'

Cleansed and purified is Pharaoh.

'On your jaw-bone I do placeth,
The Pesh-en-kef, tool of Sutekh,
Now your face is thus divided,
May you eat the grapes of power,
Words of wisdom thus you'll utter.'
Kher-Heb passes to the Sem Priest,
The Tun-tet of ostrich feather,
Waving over Pharaoh saying:

'May the roads be open to you.'
Wahabs hear their final order:
'Dress the Pharaoh in fine raiment,

SONG OF MERIKHEM

'Place the Nemes on his fine neck,
Symbol of the light of Nekheb,
Of the Hetch of Upper Khemit.

'Paint his eyes with finest metchem,
Also with the oil of u-atch.'

Khyphi incense wafts around him.
'May this fragrance reach your nostrils,
Aid you in your journey onwards.'

With his hands aloft extended,
 Sem Priest recites the many blessings:
'Sesenet neftu nedjem,
Per em rek,
Per Neteri nefruk em menet,
Ta-I nehet sedj emi,
Kheruk nedjem en mehit,
Rnpu ha-I em ankh,
En mituk.'

'May you breathe the sweet breath,
That comes forth from thy mouth,
That we behold your beauty every day,
It is our desire that you
May be rejuvenated with life
Through love of thee.'

'Di-ek eni awik kher ka-ek,

Shesepi su ankhi yemef,
I ashek reni er heh,
Ben hehif em rek.'

'Give me your hands, holding thy spirit,
That you may receive it and may live by it,
We call now upon thy name,
And it shall never fail.'

Thus is ended Pharaoh's ordeal,
Sem Priest utters a final blessing:
'Thus his mouth is ever opened,
May his voice be clear and perfect,
May his eyes now see forever,
May we rejoice now in his splendour.'

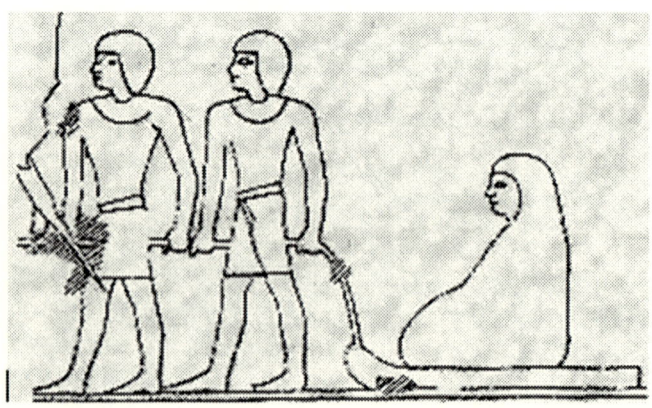

The mysterious Tekenu

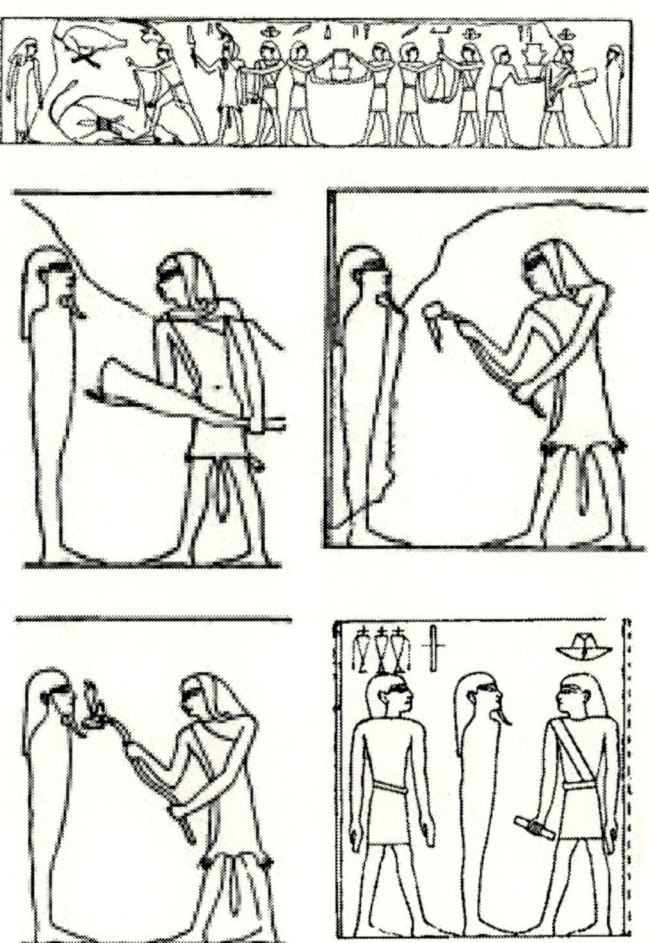

The Opening of the Mouth Ceremony

1. Slaughtering of the bull
2. Sem priest presents the thigh to pharaoh
3. Sem priest presents the adze
4. Sem priest presents the Seb-hur
5. Sem priest addressing Pharaoh in the presence of the Kher-Heb

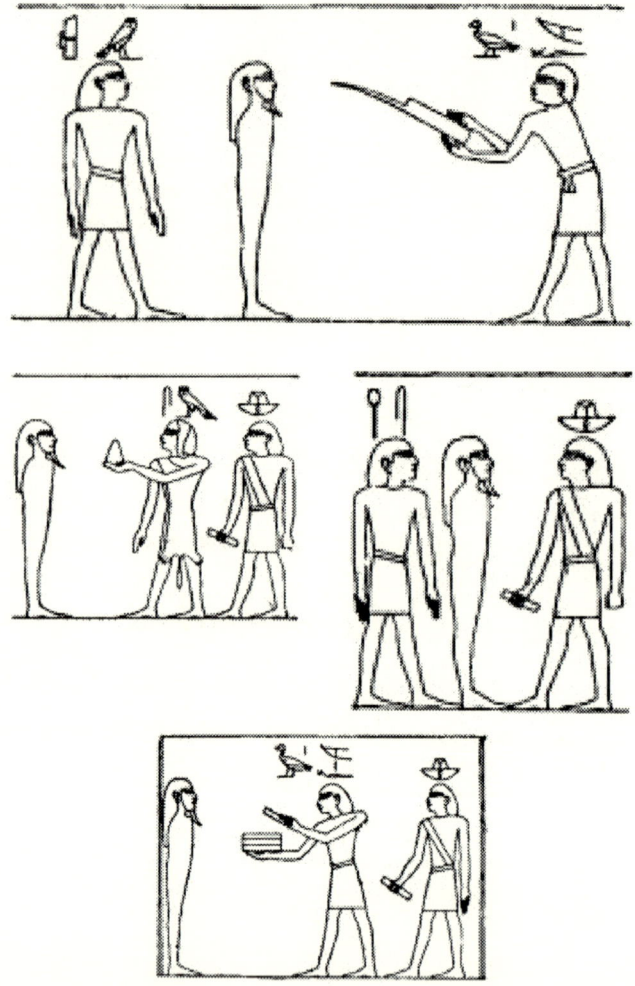

6. Sem priest opens the mouth of Pharaoh with the needle of iron – made of *smu* metal
7. Sem priest presents Pharaoh with a cone of incense
8. Sem priest utters 'You have come into purification'
9. Sem priest offers four boxes

Song of Merikhem

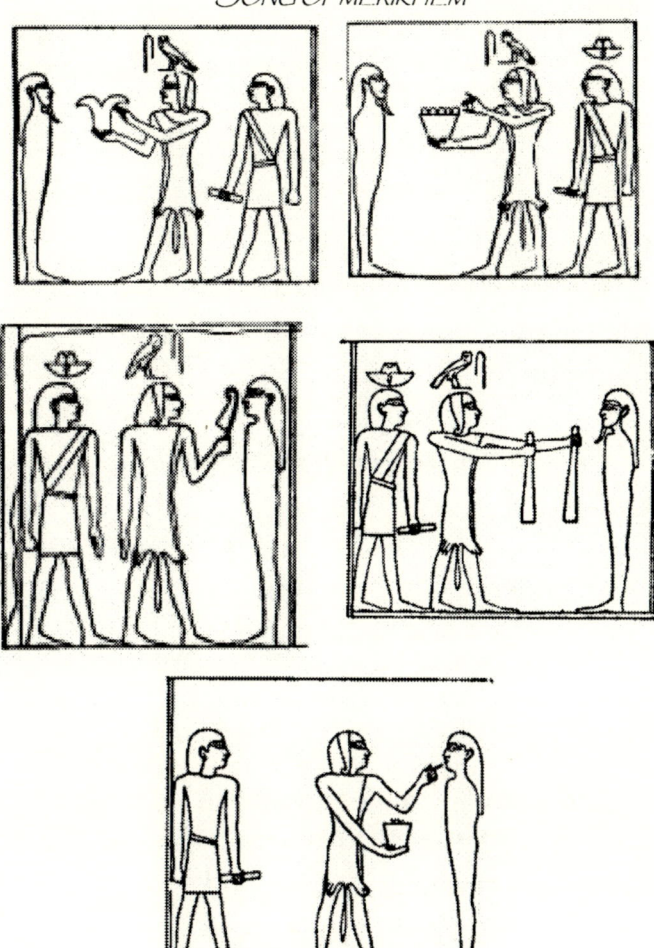

10. Sem priest lays the Peshen-Kef on Pharaoh's lips
11. Sem priest places grapes on Pharaoh's mouth
12. Sem priest waves the Tunt-tet in front of Pharaoh's mouth and eyes
13. Sem priest presenting the Nemes Bandet
14. Sem priest anointing Pharaoh with *uatch* and *mestchem*.

Chapter Nineteen
The Double Sphinx

On a moonlit night they travel,
Leave Saqqara far behind them,
Merek and Duhbe shine above them,
Meri-Khem with Kha'emwaset,
Venture on to Giza Plateau,
Known as Rostau ancient gateway.

Before them sits the Sphinx eternal,
All the mystery in his being,
All his mystery and his magick,
All his beauty in his spirit.

Meri-Khem just gazes upward,
At this wonder in the moonlight,
Asks the pilgrim 'Why sits this creature
All alone on this great plateau,
In the company of twin chapels?
Kha'emwaset, why the twinning?
Are they brothers Heru-Sutekh?'

Kha'em gazes proudly on her:
'You have guessed the oldest mystery,
When there was an Age of Twinning.'

'Re nu pert em hru.' he utters

Song of Merikhem

From the Sacred Book of Ke-hert.
'We call upon Manu and Bakhet,
Summits of the two horizons.
From the eyelids of the sunrise,
To the portals of the sunset,
Re's last journey across the heavens,
Sets the sky alight behind him.'

'To the east is Sut the Opener,
Heru-Khuti at the dawning,
Noonday he is Re-Heru-Khuti,
To the west Heru the closer,
Temu-Heru-Khuti at the setting.

'Once we had the double Sphinxes,
One faced east, the other westward.

'Deities of the two horizons,
The lion twins of ancient Khemit.
Elements of air and water,
Born of air sailing eastward,
Floating on the waters westward
Shu and Tefnut faced each other,
Representing east and westward.

'As the sun through heaven's pathway,
Re commenced his journey nightly,
Through the west to east he passeth,
To the underworld he travelled,

'Rested in the womb of Nu'it
From the Mother of the stellar
To be reborn in the morning.'

Meri thinks then answers:
'So she is mother to the solar,
Swallows up her sun child Heru,
Then gives birth to stellar Sutekh.

'Tell me of the hidden chambers,
Of the ancient Hall of Records.
Are there secret pathways buried
Under this remaining statue?
Do we have a past and future?'

'At the dawn of our beginning,'
Kha'em answered to the priestess,
'The heavens were much closer to us,
And the Gods were more familiar,
They cut out chambers in the west lion,
Under sands of time they dug them,
There was a history of Zep Tepi,
Makers of our ancient past time.'
'Have you keys that hold a secret?'
Asked the priestess looking wide-eyed.
'Are they sacred sounds to utter?'
'Ah yes,' Kha'em answered to her,
'They are multi-layered sound forms,

'That pass you through a third dimension,
On to other planes of notions,
On to other spheres of being,
To the greater and the higher.'

'May I utter then these soul sounds?'
Asks the priestess to Kha'emwaset.

Kha'em shook his head to Meri.
'There'll come another time of reason,
When all man is ripe and ready,
When his pineal gland is open.

'Revealed then, these hidden chambers,
Man will profit with this knowledge,
Thus to link man with his maker,
Linking his past-time with future,
Linking terra to the stellar.'

Kha'em gestures to the lone Sphinx:
'In the Sphinx that faces eastward,
Here we find some shallow caverns,
Also dug in ancient ages,
But were never marked with symbols,
Just left a void, a promised future.

'Then came the Græco regals,
Who made inscriptions on the sand-stone.
They were not from royal-blood Pharaohs

'Could learn nothing from their fore bears,
They wrote nothing of importance,
No great words of promised future,
Only empty prided notions.

'On the right side of this lion,
Once was seated his twin sister,
She is gone now, like her past time,
But still hidden are her chambers,
Waiting still to be re-opened,
In a time when all is golden,
This time is not that far off,
On a journey, moving closer,
Night by night the sands are shifting,
Closer are we to the real truth
As we move away from stasis.'

Chapter Twenty
Final Initiation

Brilliant in the Khemit sunshine,
From the Rostau valley gathers
Many nobles and their ladies,
Dressed up in their finest garments,
Waiting for their Pharaoh's entrance.

Many drums beat out a rhythm,
Fanfares of trumpets hail his entrance,
Of many priesthoods and their idols,
Preparing for their king's arrival.
The air is thick with kyphi incense,
Kha'emwaset walks now forward,
He is robed in full regalia,
According to his rank and station.

His crisp white tunic rustles freely,
Gathered pleats around his waistline,
Held in place by Aurichalcum,
A golden belt of red and yellow,

Hanging over his broad brown shoulders,
He wears the skin pelt of a leopard,
Worn only by the chosen, the Sem Priest.
The air is stilled at this moment,

When Pharaoh takes his first step forward,
Oiled with fragrance, and dressed in linen,
Wears the double crown, Sekhemti,
White and Red of Heru-Sutekh,
Symbols of Upper and Lower Khemit.

Across his broad chest hangs a collar,
Inlaid with many precious jewels,
Each one perfect in its setting,
Golden are his woven sandals,
Softly touching Khemit's dry sand,
In his right hand deftly carries,
Crook, flail and Uwas sceptre.

The crowds look on with jubilation.
As the king processes onward,
Walks final steps in meditation,
To the temple on the skyline,
The last rays shine upon this man-god.

Meanwhile, Meri's ushered forward,
By the Sem Priest, Kha'emwaset,
She has joined the royal company,
She traverses to the temple.

'But what trick is Kha'em playing
That I should join a king in ritual?'

SONG OF MERIKHEM

Now the hands of priests are on her,
Taking from her crown and vestments,
Clad only in her finest white robe,
Walks final steps in trepidation,
Divine and perfect is this level.

Facing her, the portal beckons,
Just before she enters solely,
Turns to face her Kha'emwaset,
From his eyes the tears are falling,
From his lips he speaks to Meri:

'I have been your guide and High Priest,
You have given truest friendship,
We have travelled far together,
Across the deserts and the wastelands,
On the Henu boat of light waves.

'I have watched you grow and blossom,
You have matched the many priestly,
And eclipsed them in their wisdom,
It is time to venture forward,
You alone will run the gamut,
All alone to prove you're mighty.
You alone will know the secrets,
And celebrate your life's renewal.

'This was Khufu's greatest temple,
Not a grave to hold his body,

Not a place of lasting sadness,
But a house to venture inwards.
Now say farewell to all your past lives.'

Meri turns to face the doorway,
Walks towards her future ending.

Darkened is the passage inside,
Her eyes adjusting to the dimness,
Upright she gropes along in dim light,
To a narrow wooden ladder,
Climbing up, then stooping forward,
Her body bending over double,
Crawling slowly like a wolf-dog,
Upward goes, but seeing nothing,
Two and seventy steps she scrambles,
Till at last she is now standing,
Lifts her gaze up to the cavern.
Before her is the corbelled gallery,
Such are these majestic layers,
That are flowing in upon her.
Peculiar sounds now filter upward,
Sounds that come from right below her,
Causing her to swoon with pleasure.

Within the bedrock of the temple,
Like giant teeth below the surface,
Forever tuning to the stellar,
They are the tuning forks of Khufu.

Song of Merikhem

Now her gaze is turning upward,
To the stairways on the sidewalls,
Centred by a deeper hallway.

Instinct tells her 'Take the left path.'
Masked and cloaked in skin of leopard,
Stands a Sem Priest waiting for her,
Beckons to the priestess, 'Follow.'
And she follows where he leads her,
Down the darkened centre hallway,
Walks on to the narrow entrance,
Through the tunnel to a chamber,
In the name of Sutekh's brother.

Hallowed is this space to Heru,
Solid granite is this chamber,
Grey-lined are the walls of this room,
In the great room's floor is centred,
White and gleaming is a coffer,
Of pure limestone it is hewn from.

In this great room stands assembled,
A priesthood waiting in position.
Await her Wahab priests of Sutekh
Shaven are their gleaming bald heads
Hairless are their well-oiled bodies,
Smelling of the sacred fragrance
Peculiar to the Lord Sutekh.
The priests are naked to the waistline,

Linen bands o'er their shoulders,
Hanging are their crisp white tunics
To their ankles hang this garment
Of linen finely spun of thread.

To the sound of drums and voices
Ringing out are strange tonations,
Causing her to swoon with pleasure.
She seems to float as chanting rises,
No more does she see the priesthood,
As she's lowered in this stone bed.

Her head is laid down to the south end,
Feet in the direction northward,
In this chasm she lays suspended,
Backward through the void she plummets,
Deeper still her body's falling,
Through the inner space of no-thing,
Then crossing o'er this greater chasm,
Feels the might of serpent current.

Within this realm are Sutekh's tunnels,
To times primeval mirrored backwards,
Into the void of formless conscience,
Plummets down into the abyss,
Sensing now a fearsome crushing,
Awaken in her ancient notions,
Where polar axis lose their meaning.
Much exalted by this magick,

Song of Merikhem

Meri slips into this dream state,
Awakens thus the ancient serpent,
Surrounds the crown part of her forehead,
Awakening powers from non-being.

Around her scarlet dust is swirling,
From a black sun never setting,
In radiant darkness comes forth Sutekh,
Incarnation of the first-one,
Reveals his secrets to this priestess.
Knowing is she of this wisdom,
She hath met the child of Nu'it.
Spake He to her words of power:
XEPER-A XEPER XEPER-U
I am He who came into being.
And in coming into being,
Created the beings,
Who came into being.

But this is only preparation,
This is not the final setting,
Raised now up, she stands erected,
Sem Priest stepping forward to her,
Leaving Heru's sacred chamber,
Returning to the corbelled gallery
In the manner she was directed.

By the left hand stair she travels.
Three and ninety are these steep steps,

Counting as she climbs, elated,
Stands and gazes upward, onward,
Taller now, and proud in bearing,
A wooden ladder leading yonder,
Seven rungs are on this ladder.

Pausing now above the gallery,
To catch her breath, she pushes onward,
Stooping once again she walks on,
Standing tall, a fleeting moment,
To stoop again before she enters.

She has walked within the adze shape,
That formed the ritual tool of Sutekh,
Walked the path of Ursa Major,
Has become the tool of Shaitan.
Enters this huge, and inner sanctum
Of Lord Sutekh, child of Nu'it.

Chamber walls of black lined granite,
Ring with vowel sounds from the many,
In this great room's floor is centred,
A large red coffer, empty, ready.

She seems to float as chanting rises,
Lowered again into this stone bed,
Positioned is her empowered body,
As her head is south positioned,
Feet in the direction northward;

Song of Merikhem

In this chasm she's suspended,
While the Sem Priest begins a'chanting,
Four Wahab priests stand at the corners,
Hands placed on the sacred coffer,
Making vowel sounds for the rebirth,
Sounds that penetrate her being,
No more does she see the priesthood,
Altered states of mind she's sensing.

The coffer now begins to vibrate,
Exciting crystals in the granite
Now white powder falls upon her,
Causing walls to turn transparent,
With mingled sounds of much intoning.
Her body now is in suspension,
No longer do her veins hold red blood,
She is filled with such vibration,
As she's raised to cosmic levels.

Chamber shafts turn into tunnels,
Each emits a special tuning,
Sobdet now is beckoning to her.
A blue white sun that now envelops,
Pulling her to venture upward,
Blue-tinged rays now flood the chamber,
Scattering light within her being,
She is now the milk of stardust.

Looking down its spiral structure,

Crosses now the stellar ocean,
Still in sight is the greater temple,
Crystal glowing in the vortex,
Another tunnel opens further,
Spinning tumbling falling through it,
Towards a brilliant red corona,
To a different time and order.

Then before her is The Great Bear,
Alkaid, Alioth and Miza,
Alcor, Phecda follow Megrez,
Then comes Merak and now Dhube,
Wondrous is their star formation,
Suspended in the outer limits.

All the stars of night look at them,
Hanging in most perfect friendship,
Now these very stars in heaven,
Make her tremble with such fervour.
Closer now she moves among them,
Much mystery is now told to her,
Listens to this multi-format,
Listens to the words of stardust,
Then a voice is heard, a whisper,
Coming from the starry distance,
Coming from the empty vastness.

Wrapt in visions, lost in dreaming,
'I see the broad red stellar pathway,

Song of Merikhem

Pathway of the gods and shadows,
Now I hear a voice that calls me,
I hear his voice boom through the starlight.'

Now a hand is thus extended,
'Walk now straight across the stardust
To the kingdom of hereafter.'
Gone now is her fear and anguish,
As great Sutekh stands before her
As Meri-Khem goes to her being.

Explanatory notes on the Heb Sed Two Festival

For centuries, since the Great Pyramid's chambers have been opened to the many visitors throughout the ages, archaeologists and Egypt-ologists have confused everyone with false notions of some fantastic burial place for the long deceased King Khufu.

Since no evidence has been discovered to support this idea of a final resting place for the king, I put it to you, that the so-called King and Queen's Chambers were used for another, and more significant purpose, other than burial.

We must first look at the Heb Sed Festival of renewal, and re-birth of the Pharaoh. This highly charged event would take place every 30 years of the king's reign, but in some of the earlier dynasties, it was celebrated more frequently.

An open space, such as the grand arena in

front of Zoser's pyramid at Saqqara, was prepared in respect for the two mighty deities, Set and Horus. This was known as the Heb Sed Court, flanked on both sides with the chapels of the Upper and Lower Egyptian gods of each nome.

The king would run in the open space between the two rows of shrines dressed alternatively in the insignia colours of white for Upper, and red for Lower Egypt. This ritual race around the 'field' was repeated four times as the ruler of the South, and four times as ruler of the North.

This was indeed a very public occasion, witnessed by Pharaoh's subjects who not only regarded this as a great spectacle, but also put great store in the safe delivery of their king as he ran the 'gamut'.

But the true test of Pharaoh's strength was not to be physical. This test was indeed an act of rebirth and renewal of mind and spirit, and the ritual setting would have been the great pyramid of Khufu. The king would be prepared in the usual manner i.e. in his stately regalia, and together with a retinue of priests and attendees, he would make his way from the valley of the Sphinx, up the flag-stoned causeway, to the entrance of the Great Pyramid. Pharaoh would then be relieved of his cape, sceptres and crowns, and remained dressed only in a short white linen kilt. After priestly blessings, he would then venture alone, through the pyramid entrance bearing the hieroglyph letter of the god Hapuy, and into the dimly lit corridor.

If we look at a cross section of the Great Pyramid of Khufu, we will notice that the passageways and shafts leading to the two chambers resemble the constellation of Ursa Major. We must also look at the corresponding link between the shape of the adze, fashioned out of the painstaking gathering of tektites from the surrounding desert, which were later smelted down to make this instrument.

As Pharaoh made his way up through the pyramid, he would then be reduced to the very form of the constellation of The Plough, which is also representative of the god Set. In this doubling, crawling and walking phase, the king proceeds to the so-called King's Chamber by way of the left-hand stairs up through the corbelled gallery.

For argument sake, I will call this room the Chamber of Set. There is nothing inside this great space, but for a large sarcophagus of red granite, the orientation from the longest sides, south to north. The walls and floor are of black granite.

Priests would be present to aid Pharaoh as he was placed in the sarcophagus, head to the south and feet to the north, which signifies the position of the pole star in the north.

After the chanting of prayers the Sem priest would then signal the commencement of the ritualistic ordeal Pharaoh would be put through. Four priests would position themselves at either corner of the sarcophagus, and placing their fingertips on the edge of the coffer, would intone specifics vowel sounds. According to John Reid, a specialist in the study of Sonics: 'When certain sounds are played in close proximity to granite, these sound frequencies excite the crystals within the stone, which makes them resonate'.

Given that the entire chamber and sarcophagus is of granite, this would have brought about a physical, mental and spiritual change within the body and mind of the king. His very being would be saturated with sound. His limbs and vessels would be tingling due to the vibrations of this deliberate orchestration of tones, each priest emitting a prescriptive dose.

At a particular point, the Sem priest would indicate to the Wahabs, to gently remove Pharaoh from the coffer, and in a backwards or reversed mode, the king would leave the

SONG OF MERIKHEM

Set: The Return

Chamber of Set. He would be fully prepared for his next phase of rebirth and renewal, which would take place in the room below, which I will call, the Chamber of Horus.

Walking backwards down the right hand side of the corbelled gallery, reversing along a corridor between the double stairway, bending double and still in reverse, Pharaoh would enter this next chamber. He would not see the priesthood, but would be aware of yet more chanting and intoning of carefully chosen notes which once again resonate through the granite. The walls of this chamber are lined with pale grey granite and in the centre of the floor is placed a gleaming white limestone sarcophagus of similar proportions to that of the coffer in the Chamber of Set.

Once again Pharaoh is guided and placed in the coffer. His emotions run high as he is plunged into the great abyss of the celestial waters. In trance, his body sleeps, but his soul is awake. It is active on its own plane; the body is in the background of a different matter. This mind-altering state has rid him of his fragile body, as he is absorbed into the realms of non-being. He is awakened to the super consciousness of that which IS, and everything that is portrayed, is of the events of the inner world by way of a mirroring. His conditions of focus are being determined by these emotional states.

He has been subjected to the very force of the Primum Mobile, and with this seventh ray of consciousness he has received Complete Initiation into the 'living death'. Thus, he has achieved the freedom of the spirit brought through to the plane of matter. He is free, empowered, and stands taller and greater amongst his fellow Man.

In those days, a Pharaoh was a man alone. He would have had the council of his Sem and the input of the Vizier etc., but after a Heb Sed festival of rebirth and renewal, this would make him supra human.

The very design of the Great Pyramid sets a platform for a magnificent and mind-altering stage for a special event. One can only enter this great monument today, to realise that there is something very special and poignant about the peculiar design quality of these tunnels and shafts, all hidden from public view. Who else but the ancient Egyptians would fashion a tunnel on the god Set's constellation of Ursa Major?

As we enter this great mound of calculated pieces of stone, our body twists and doubles up, we crawl and walk tall as did the pharaohs of old. We reach the inner sanctum, totally exhausted, and stand over an empty granite box where the king would have been plunged into his own kind of oblivion. We too are laid waste in this empty room, and some of us wonder what it's all about. Then, as we make our way down again to the outside world, we find that secretly and subliminally, the pyramid has given us back something else, in return for the energy we gave it, to breathe new life into the Great Tunnels of Set.

Glossary

Abju: Ancient Egyptian name for *Abydos*.

Abydos: Greek form of *Abju*.

Abyss: The great gulf or void that constitutes the separation of individual consciousness from its universal source. To Cross the Abyss, or transcend the world of subject and object and resolve the antinomies of mundane consciousness.

Adze: Ancient ritual object made from iron tektites: it was fashioned in the shape of the constellation *Ursa Major, The Great Bear* or *Plough*. This also symbolised the god *Set*.

Akhet: Season of the inundation in the ancient Egyptian calendar, heralded by the rising of Sirius, the dog-star called Sobdet.

Alcor: Star in the constellation of Ursa Major.

Alkaid: Star in the constellation of Ursa Major.

Amenti: A mythological domain of the dead on the western shore of the Nile.

Amon-em-het: 12th Dynastic Pharaohs.

Amon: Ancient local god of Thebes whose name means 'hidden one', or 'the Great Cackler'.

Amonhotep1: Founding builder of Luxor Temple.

Andjeti: God in anthropomorphic form originally worshipped in the mid-Delta in the Lower Egyptian nome.

Ankh: (or crux ansata) The symbol of eternal life in ancient Egypt.

Antef: Early feudal warlord who later became one of the early Pharaohs of Egypt.

Anubis: Greek form of Anpu - dog god deity of the dead.

Apep: see *Apophis.*

Apis: the sacred bull, a theophany of the Ptah-Sokar cult at Memphis.

Apophis: A giant mythical serpent with mystical powers who was the enemy of the sun-god Re.

Asar: Ancient Egyptian for *Osiris.* There are over one hundred names of gods that start with the prefix 'Asar'.

Athyr: Third month of the season of *Akhet* - winter - inundation.

Atum: Sun-god and creator of the universe. The name *Atum,* carries the idea of 'totality' in the sense of an ultimate and unalterable state of perfection.

Aurichalcum: Mysterious red flecked gold, thought to have originated from the mythical Atlantis.

Bakhet: God of the East and summit of the two horizons.

Behdet: ancient Egyptian for Edfu.

Benenet: Ancient mound of earth that sprang out of the first waters.

Chaos: The primal substance that is, paradoxically, by no means substantial, out of which the illusion of formless primordial Matter appears to rise.

Crook: Emblem of sovereignty and divinity.

Deshert: Red crown of Lower Egypt in the North.

Djed: the ancient Egyptian symbol for stability.

Djedu: Ancient town in the Delta, and Nome region of the ancient god, Andjety.

Djinns: Spirit form lower than angels.

Dhube: Star in the constellation of Ursa Major.

Edfu: Greek form. Called Behdet by the ancient Egyptians meaning 'Exhaltation of Horus'.

Enki: (or *Ea*) 'Lord of the Earth' - God of Mesopotamia.

Eridu: Cult centre of Enki triad, located at the head of the present Persian Gulf.

Esna: Cult centre for god Khnemu and goddess Nebtu'u.

Fayum: Modern name of Ta-she and Sher-resy.

Flail: Emblem of sovereignty and dignity.

Geb: Earth-god and president of the divine tribunal on the kingship according to the Osirian mythology.

Giza: A plateau south of modern Cairo see *Rostau*.

Great Bear: Another name for Ursa Major.

Great Eternal: The un-manifest made pure existence.

Hadit: Chaldean form of *Set*.

Hapuy: God of the annual Nile inundation. The god is shown in human form with aquatic plants on his head.

Haroerus: Elder Horus in the Osirian Pantheon Group.

Heb Sed: An elaborate ceremony of the king's Coronation: his '*Sed*' festival or jubilee and ultimate burial, were twice repeated with the different insignia, architecture and customs of Upper and Lower Egypt. The ceremony of the 'Running of Apis' appears to have been closely associated with the Sed Festival, but it seems more likely to have been originally a celebration of the festival called the 'Birth of the god *Sed*'. The entire nation was deeply concerned with the celebration of these important rites.

The festival usually took place thirty years after the king's accession to the throne. However, according to the evidence of the Palermo Stone, the *Sed* festival was celebrated by some of the archaic kings repeatedly, and at much shorter intervals than the accepted thirty year period. In order to celebrate this important festival, a special building was erected, called a *Sed* Pavilion. This included a Throne Room and a Robing Room in which the king changed his garments and insignia according to the various double rites connected with the two lands.

But most important was the *Heb-Sed* Court, flanked on both sides with the chapels of the Upper and Lower Egyptian gods of each *nome*. The king would run in the open space between the two rows of shrines dressed alternatively in the insignia colours of white for Upper, and red for Lower Egypt. This ritual race around the 'field' was repeated four times as the ruler of the South, and four times as ruler of the North. It is suggested that the 'field' represented Egypt and the ritual race perhaps signified to all those present, his claim as possessor of the land. To this was added the further impetus for national fertility - his actions made the land fruitful and productive.

Hedjet: White crown of Upper Egypt in the South.

Hem-Neter: A title given to one who serves all the Neters.

Henu boat: A magickal boat that was never meant to sail on water, but was driven by light.

Heru-Khuti: Ancient Egyptian god of the East.

Heru-Sutekh: Twin form of *Horus* and *Set*.

Heru: Ancient Egyptian for *Horus*.

Hetch: Light or brilliance coming from *Nekheb*.

Hidden One: A reference given to *Amon* - his form cannot be known.

Horus: Greek form of *Heru*.

Ineb-Hedj: An ancient lime-stone wall built by Aha also known as Menes.

Ir-Nkhn: Ancient Egyptian for Nekhen.

Iry-Pat: Sacred kings who originated from Sumer.

Isa: Ancient form of *Isis*.

Isis: Greek form of *Isa*.

Isit-Nefert: 2nd wife of Rameses II, and mother of Kha'emwaset.

Ka: Ancient Egyptian term for a spiritual essence.

Karnak: Ancient name, Nesut-Towi, 'Throne of The Two Lands' and site of the temple god Amon.

Kha'emwaset: Ramesses II' favourite son and High priest of Ptah in *Men-nefer*.

Khem: A name applied to Egypt as the black or red land. The black or red Nilotic mud that literally formed Egypt.

Khemit: see *Khem*.

Khenta-menthes: Ancient dog-god, and other form of Set in Abydos.

Khepresh: Great war crown.

Kher-Heb: Priest, lector and master of mortuary rituals.

K-hert: Sacred Book of the Dead.

Khoiak: Fourth month in the season of *Akhet*.

Khonsu: His original name means 'navigator' associated with the moon and healing.

Khufu: Reigned between 2551 - 2528 - Old Kingdom. He was the Pharaoh who built the Great Pyramid.

Kom el-Ahmar: Modern name for *Nekhem*.

Labyrinth: A complicated irregular structure with

many passages all designed to create confusion.

Luxor: Modern Arabic name for Thebes.

Mammon: Regarded as the god of wealth and influence.

Manu: God of the West and summit of the two horizons.

Mastaba: Term given to the step pyramid of Zoser.

Medula Oblongata: A bundle of nerves in a formation known as the 'decussation of the pyramids'.

Megrez: Star in the constellation of Ursa Major.

Menes: Also known as Aha.

Men-Nefer: Ancient Egyptian form of *Memphis*.

Mentuhotep: 11th Dynasty king.

Merak: Star in the constellation of Ursa Major.

Mer-wer: Lake at Fayum.

Meshenti: Regal crown of Set.

Meska: Skin of a bull.

Messeh: Sacred oil of the crocodile used for anointing of Kings and Queens even to this day.

Mesxet: Star in the constellation of Ursa Major.

Metchem: Sacred eye unguent used in 'Opening

of Mouth Ceremony'.

Mut: Goddess and consort of *Amon*.

Mystery Play: Sacred play of Osiris performed in Abydos in the ancient month of Khoaik.

Naqada: North of Thebes, ancient cult centre of Set.

Narmer: One of the last pre-dynastic kings associated with the unification of Upper and Lower Egypt.

Natron: Ancient name, net-jeryt - 'belonging to god' used mainly for embalming and purification. Found at the Wadi Natrun north of modern day Cairo.

Nefertum: God of the primeval lotus blossom and son to *Ptah* and *Sekhmet* triad of *Memphis*.

Nekheh: Re.

Nekhbet: Vulture goddess of *Nekheb* upholding the king's sway in Upper Egypt.

Nekhen: Now modern *Kom el-Ahmar*.

Nemes: Band or fillet, symbol of the 'light of Nekheb' - Set.

Nephthi: (or Nephthys in Greek) Fifth child of *Nut* and *Geb*, according to the *Osirian* pantheon mythology.

Nephthys: Greek form of Nebt-Hut.

Nesut-Towi: see *Karnak*.

Neter: Ancient Egyptian for a god.

Nilometric Cubit: Ancient measures that are featured in the Luxor Temple as black stones symbolizing Set.

Nomes: Pharaonic Egypt was divided into forty-two administrative districts, or nomes. Each nome had principal deities.

Nu: (or *Nun*) God personifying the primeval waters out of which emerged the creator-god. Nu is the 'father to all gods' but this emphasises only his unrivalled antiquity as an element of the Egyptian cosmos - in terms of importance, he is superseded by the creator sun-god *Atum*.

Nun: A being of Ancient Egypt, believed to symbolize the primeval watery abyss.

Nuit: 'Infinite Space and the Infinite Stars thereof'. In a metaphysical sense, *Nuit* is the Continuum of paradise that results from the resolution of mundane being into the elements of non-being. *Nuit* is represented as a human female form arched over the earth as in the Stele of Revealing. In a more specialised and magickal sense, she is the complement of *Set*. She is North, and compares with *Set*, whose opposite is *Horus* in the South.

Nut: (see *Nuit*).

Ombos: The *Set*-worshipping tribes occupying a large area in Upper Egypt called *Ombos*. This area was also famous for the mining of gold.

Opening of Mouth Ceremony: A long and complex rite in which links were established or renewed with the soul of the departed king. It also has very strong Setian implications.

Opet: Patron goddess of eastern Thebes. Also the name given to the *Opet* temple in *Karnak*.

Ophidian: A member of the serpentine order of reptiles.

Osirian: A follower of *Osiris*.

Osiris: Greek form of *Asar* and *Wasir*.

Osireion: A mysterious subterranean building situated behind the Great Temple of Sety I.

Peribsen: A king of the 2nd dynasty.

Pesh-en-kef: Associated with Set's forked tail. Usually made from a salmon-pinkish stone called carnelian, and commonly used in *Opening of Mouth Ceremony*.

Pharaoh: Derived from *Har-Iu*, which means the Coming Son of a two-fold nature, and of the two *IU* Houses.

Phecda: Also known as Phad, star in the constellation of Ursa Major.

Proyet: A season of sowing – Springtime.

Ptah: God of *Memphis* and part of the triad of *Nerfertum* and *Sekhmet*.

Ptah-Sokar: Another name for *Ptah* associated with mortuary statues.

Ptolemaic: Graeco-Egyptians.

Quema: Sacred incense to *Set* from *Nekhen*.

Ra: see Re.

Rameses II: 3rd king of the 19th dynasty and greatest of all the non-royal blood Kings of ancient Egypt. He was part of a long succession of Setian followers.

Re: Creator sun-god of *Khenemu* (or *Heliopolis*).

Re-Heru-Khuti: God of the noon-day sun.

Rostau: Necropolis containing the pyramid fields – was known as the *Duat*. A gateway, or entrance.

Royal placenta bundle: The king's placenta, called the 'Sacred Bundle of Life', is taken and preserved at the time of his birth. It is kept wrapped in the form of a kidney shape, for the entirety of the king's life. Ceremonially carried on a high pole by the *Sem* priest at all festive occasions, it is buried with the king at the point of his death (see *Sem Priest*).

Sacred Bundle: see *Royal Placenta Bundle.*

Sahu: Ancient Egyptian name for Orion.

Salamander: Elemental spirit living within fire.

Saqqara: A plateau overlooking the ancient city of *Men Nefer*. Its vast courtyard or 'field' was used for the celebration of the *Heb-Sed* festival.

Seb-Hur: Instrument of Anubis, used in Opening of Mouth Ceremony. It symbolized Horus - The Great Star, and god of the South.

Sekhmet: Wife to *Ptah* and mother to *Nerfertum*. Part of the triad of Memphis. She is also associated with healing of the bones and battle.

Sekhmet-Montu: War god of Thebes and linked with

Sekhmet: Lion-headed goddess, consort of *Ptah*.

Sekhemti: The Red and White crowns of Upper and Lower Egypt produced the Double Crown, a combination of the two emblems.

Sem Priest: the chief or High Priest. He also held the first and most honourable station as the one who offered sacrifice and libation in the temple - the highest post. He appears to have been called 'the prophet' and his title in the hieroglyphic legends is '*Sem*'. The *Sem Priest* was the only person who was lawfully allowed to kill the king if he proved unable to continue to rule the land of *Khem*. This would be as a result of not being able to meet the test of the *Heb-Sed*, becoming gravely ill being or perhaps mortally wounded in battle. The most famous *Sem Priest* was *Setne Kha'emwaset*, favourite and most royal son of *Rameses II*. Apart from having the responsibility for arranging the many *Heb-Sed* festivals for his father the king, this particular priest was probably the first Egyptologist of those times to actually set about restoring the *Saqqara* plateau. This would have included the many pyramids and temples, some of which were already two thousand years old.

Serapeum: see *Usir-Hapuy*.

Set: (or Sut) The primordial god of the ancient Egyptians; no earlier god exists in the recorded history of the present human race. The word 'soot' is derived from this incalculably ancient name. *Set* is also the prototype of *Shaitan* or *Satan*, God of the South whose star is *Sothis*. *Set*, or *Sut* (literally meaning 'black') is the chief colour (or *kala*) of *Set*. Black indicates the dark mysteries of this god which were originally enacted in the underworld, 'netherworld', or Amonta. The god is Lord of Amonta, or 'hidden land' - in other words, Hell. Hell is the epitome of sub-consciousness, and therefore, of the True Will or Hidden Sun, the *sun* behind the *sun* symbolised by the *Star of Set, Sothis.* (see also *Shaitan).*

Setian: A follower, or worshiper of the god *Set.*

Setereion: Author's re-name of *Osireion.*

Sety l: 2nd king of the 19th dynasty, and father to *Rameses II.*

Shaitan: The god of the Yezidi, who personified the star *Sothis* or *Sobdet.* The rising of this star heralded the inundation of the river Nile which brought blessed relief to a sun-stricken land.

Shaman: An early priest who would adopt the guise of an animal by wearing its skin, horns and tail. The carrying of totem animals, later developed into the standards bearing the emblems of the popular deities of the regions, or *nomes.*

Shemu: Harvest season.

Sher-resy: Ancient name for Fayum.

Shu: God of sunlight and air. *Shu* takes a human form wearing a plume (which is also the hieroglyphics for his name) on his head, and with his arms raised supporting the sky-goddess *Nut,* whom he holds apart from her consort the earth god, *Geb.*

Smayu Net Set: Ancient name for the 'Companions of Set'.

Sobek: Crocodile god whose cult centre was Fayum. He was also the patron deity of many of the kings of the 13th dynasty.

Sokar: Hawk god of the Memphite necropolis, also known as 'lord of the mysterious region'.

Sokaris: see Sokar.

Sothis: see *Sirius*.

Sphinx: Form of a recumbent lion with the head of a royal personage.

Sut: Means 'The Opener' - and *Horus* who 'Shuts' or 'Closes' *Sut* as the brother of the Sun, *Horus*.

Sutekh: Another name for *Set*.

Sut-Typhon: The taunt flung at the *Sut-Typhonians* by the Osirians, was 'Orphan', intending to brand them as Fatherless in a religious sense because they worshipped only the Mother and Child, who became looked upon as the Harlot and the Bastard. The irony is that it was accepted that the mother of the Christ-child experienced an immaculate conception.

Talisman: A charm or amulet, an object supposedly capable of working magick.

Ta-Wer: Exalted Land.

Tefnut: Primeval goddess personifying moisture. She is the female consort of *Shu*.

Tekenu: Mysterious figure in a hooded sack-shaped garment that was always present at Opening of Mouth Ceremonies.

Telluric current: Earth energy.

Temu: Cosmic god.

Temu-Heru-Khuti: God of the setting sun.

Terra Firma: Earth.

Thebes: Greek form of modern day Luxor.

Tun-tet: Ostrich feather, used in Opening of Mouth Ceremony.

Two Horizons: see *Sut-Har*.

U-atch: Sacred oil used for the nostrils of the dead in the *Opening of Mouth Ceremony*.

Udi-mu: A king of the First Dynasty. He is always depicted wearing the white crown '*Hedjet*', and dressed in a closely fitted garment. This apparel was to be copied later, when depicting the god *Osiris*. The reign of *Udi-mu* pre-dates the introduction of the Osirian mythology and religion, as this king's sacred animal was the baboon i.e. *Thoth* or *Djehuti* in conjunction with the Apis.

Undine: Female water spirit.

Ur-Egypt: Term given to early pre-dynastic Egypt.

Ur-Hekau: 'The Mighty One of Spells'. The Great Magick Power represented the thigh or khepsh of the Goddess Nut, in which the star dwells. The term *ur-hekau* connects this light with hekt, or heket, the lunar ophidian (serpent) current represented by the frog, lizard, hare, ape, hyena and other lunar symbols of change, or magickal transformation. The ancient Egyptians used a magick wand which they called *Ur-Hekau*. It was in the form of a ram-headed snake. This was the symbol of the 'Living Word' that had its origins in feminine nature. The ram was a symbol of Amon, and also the Age of Aries, the Hidden God carried over from the previous æon when the crocodile was the zoötype of *Set*, the god born of the thigh of *Typhon*. The custodian of this magickal wand would be the *Sem Priest*.

Ursa Major: Is the constellation of the Thigh which typified the birthplace of Light in the Dark of the Abyss. The Goddess of the seven stars of *Ursa Major* with *Set* the Dog-star as the annual proclaimer of the Goddess, were reflected terrestrially as the sixteen sanctuaries of *Osiris* - eight in Upper Egypt, and eight in Lower Egypt. *Nut* was typified celestially by this constellation. The seven stars of this complex symbolised Night or *Typhon* and her offspring, to which at a later time was added her first male child, *Set* or *Sothis*. It is interesting to note that the *adze* is shaped in the form of *Ursa Major*.

Usir-Hapuy: Ancient Egyptian name for *Serapeum*.

Uwas sceptre: A sceptre made in the likeness of the god *Set*. This emblem of dignity was carried by the Pharaoh during ceremonial and state occasions, regardless of whether the king was a follower of this deity.

Wadjet: Was the cobra goddess of Buto and the guardian and preserver of royal authority over Lower Egypt.

Wahab: Were the lowest rank of priests in the temple. Nevertheless, they were necessary for the daily working of the temple. All of the priesthood were very conscious about their diet, and in general, 'the priests abstained from most sorts of pulse, mutton and swine's flesh'; and in their more solemn purifications, even excluded salt from their meals. They were as strict about their ablutions as in their diet. They bathed twice a day, and twice during the night, and some were so strict, they would only wash themselves with the water which had been tasted by the ibis. Every third day they would shave their head and entire body. They spared no pains when it came to the promotion of cleanliness. Grand ceremonies of purification took place in preparation to their fasts, many of which lasted from seven to forty-two days. Some would even fast for an even longer period. During this time they abstained entirely from meat, herbs and vegetables. All other extra indulgences were put aside. However, the priests enjoyed great privileges. They paid no taxes, no part of their income was used for the necessary expenses of life, any land they owned was free from all duties and a state allowance of corn was given to them as well as provision from the public stores.

Wasir: Ancient Egyptian form of Osiris.

Wep-wa-wet: 'Opener-of-ways' appears originally to have been a war god who led the king to battle, but in later times he became a god of the dead, and was eventually assimilated to *Anubis*. He is depicted as a wolf standing on a *nome* standard. He is also the original and chief deity of *Abju*, a realm later to be usurped by *Osiris*.

Zep Tepi: A mysterious form of the 'first ones' in ancient Egypt.

Zoser: the second king of the 3rd Dynasty circa 2630 - 2611, son of Kha-Sekhemwy a Setian king.

SONG OF MERIKHEM

The Bull of Ombos:
Seth & Egyptian Magick II
by Mogg Morgan

£12.99, ISBN 1869928873
356pp, 80 b&w illustrations

Naqada is a sleepy little town in Upper Egypt, that gives its name to a crucial period in the prehistory of Egypt. In 1895, William Matthew Flinders Petrie, the 'father' of Egyptian archaeology, stumbled upon a necropolis, belonging to a very ancient city of several thousand inhabitants. With Petrie's usual luck, he'd made yet another archaeological find of seismic proportions – not just an ancient city a quarter the size of Ur in Mesopotamia, a rare enough find, but the capital of the earliest state established in Egypt! Petrie's fateful walk through the desert led him to a lost city, known to the Greeks as Ombos, the Citadel of Seth. Seth, the Hidden God, once ruled in this ancient place before it was abandoned to the sands of the desert. All this forbidden knowledge was quickly reburied in academic libraries, where its stunning magical secrets had lain, largely unrevealed, for more than a century - until now.

This book is for all Egyptophiles as well as anyone with an interest in the archaic roots of magick and the sabbatic craft.

Contents: Gold in the desert / Sethians and Osirians compared / Cannibalism / Temple of Seth / Seth's Town / Seth as Bull of Ombos / Hathor / The names of Seth / Animals of Seth / Seth - the red ochre god / Seth and Horus / Opening the mouth / Seven / The Boat / Heka & Hekau / Magical activities / Cakes of Light / Magick as use and misuse of the funeral rite / Re-emergence of the Hidden God / Five useful Appendices / Extended bibliography / Glossary

**Visit our website: www.mandrake.uk.net
or call for a catalogue on +44 (01)865 243671
email mandrake@mandrake.uk.net
write to: PO Box 250, Oxford, OX1 1AP (UK)**

Printed in the United States
200036BV00006B/19-21/A